MONERGY
EXPERIENCE THE ULTIMATE ENERGY OF MONEY

ROBERT M. FISHER

MONERGY
EXPERIENCE THE ULTIMATE ENERGY OF MONEY

ROBERT M. FISHER

Cover and book design by Dave Bricker.

ISBN: 978-0-9981821-4-8

To those who aspire
to be themselves

Monergy

CONTENTS

Monergy

PREFACE

The world has always been in flux, but the pace of change has accelerated. Constant connectivity is the name of the game, and the challenges you face as an engaged member of society are staggering. You are expected to constantly learn new things, and to process that information quickly. But everyone needs to relax and pace themselves, and today's challenges require a belief system that accommodates this, and more.

It doesn't matter whether the economic system is amped up capitalism or a more egalitarian approach.

This book demonstrates that despite outward appearances, energy controls not just making and spending money wisely, but the means for a peaceful, happy, and fulfilled life — a life where you don't have to sell your soul to achieve your dreams.

Learning how to access that energy is what this book is about.

Monergy

INTRODUCTION

Monergy is a made-up word, but it represents the energy that surrounds making and spending money. This book explores how your own energy has sabotaged your financial goals. It introduces a new moneymaking consciousness based upon energy.

Money is being flashed in your face like never before, but the glitzy illusion of wealth can distort its real value. It's not enough to just blindly say, "I want more money." Learn about the subtle energy effects of moneymaking, because energy is fluid and controls everything. The energy you apply toward making money affects every other area of your life, whether you like it or not.

This book explores the energy surrounding money with honesty and depth. You will learn the energy components that are most likely to get you desired wealth, use it effectively, and sustain it over time. Don't be bound by past mistakes. Don't obsess about what's next. Create a prosperous future with your present moment efforts, regardless of whatever tragedy is playing out on the current news.

Be prepared to look inward, to struggle, to be skeptical, and maybe even be ecstatic.

Enjoy the ride.

— Robert Fisher

PART I

ENERGY EXPOSURE

Chapter 1

The Power of Energy

Have you ever noticed that when your energy changes, it affects everything that you do, including the ability to make money? You probably thought these shifts in your life were entirely random, and that you were never able to connect them in a meaningful way. You can now. This book will explain how your own energy either makes you rich or keeps you poor.

I discovered these connections by working as a lawyer and as a real estate developer in New York City. My first big example of this happened when I was a twenty-five year-old lawyer in a will contest. My client, Ruth, was a beneficiary under a will where the estate was worth several million dollars. She was a good friend of the decedent, Sally, a rich and eccentric old Swedish woman who had lived in an East Side Manhattan townhouse. Ned was the trustee under the will, and also a beneficiary and high-powered establishment type. It soon became clear that Ned was trying to steal the entire estate for himself. Under the cloak of white glove civility, he had no intention of letting the other beneficiaries, including my client, have a thing. What is the "cloak of white glove civility?" It is a very particular combination of appearance, position, and so-called breeding, designed to intimidate and control others; it is sometimes used as a smokescreen to steal the whole pie.

The problem Ned and my client had was that the original will, which gave Ned so much control over the estate, was superseded by a later will that left *everything* to Sally's maid, who had only worked for Sally during the last three months of her life — a very suspicious situation with Stephen King-like intrigue.

A will contest ensued in Manhattan Surrogate's Court, which administers wills and estates. Ned's high-powered lawyers were politically well connected. They attempted a two-pronged attack. First, they claimed the maid's will was not valid based on incompetence, or undue influence. After that will was eliminated, they planned to destroy my client's claim based upon a trumped-up technicality.

The will contest went into high gear. Over the next six months, through numerous conferences and depositions, I picked up various signals about the participants and the court, itself. Ned's lawyer, who was about twice my age, treated me as though I were an undesirable element that had stuck to his shoe. He took every opportunity to belittle my client's claim and myself. The maid's lawyer was condescending too; he was also well known in Surrogate's Court. Further, the attorney for New York State's interest in the estate was an elder statesman type, well connected and polished, who I thought might be on my side, but I was later proved wrong. Additionally, the Surrogate Court and its staff were demeaning to me, which I attributed to my novice status.

The court was a club that wouldn't let me in. An interesting thing happened whenever I appeared at a conference in Surrogate's Court on this case. The surrogate would invite the other three participating attorneys into her chambers and would literally shut the door in my face. They appeared as greedy coconspirators carving up a pie that excluded me. Their collective energy was extremely negative.

Although the surrogate could bar me from her chambers, Ned's lawyer had to make an actual motion to dismiss my client's claim. I sensed he was going to do it soon, and sure enough he did. At the same time, he threw some money at the maid so she would release her claim to the whole estate.

Ned's attorney invited me to his plush Park Avenue office before the hearing date for that motion. The attorney representing New York State's interest in the estate was also present. I had sometimes thought the attorney for New York State admired my spunk, but he ultimately sided with Ned's attorney to knock out my client's claim. (This well respected elder attorney was forced to resign his official position several years later due to an embezzlement scandal.)

Ned's lawyer sat behind his gigantic desk in the comfort of his white glove law firm. He offered a paltry sum for my client to withdraw her claim. The attorney for New York State urged me to accept the money, and insisted that my client had no real claim to any part of the estate. Of note: while Ned's attorney was sitting behind his desk making his insulting offer, he deliberately picked his nose while looking at me — a sign of utter disrespect. I rejected his ungenerous offer, even though my client's case was not that strong.

A few years earlier, I had begun to practice meditation. I would sit with my palms facing up, and would either make my mind go blank, or visualize things I wanted to happen. I would perform this exercise, which involved being completely motionless, for fifteen minutes in the morning and fifteen minutes in the evening. Even though I was only

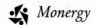

twenty-five, there was much that I wanted to happen. I was hopeful that a meditation practice would help.

The hearing date arrived, and I went to Surrogate's Court, which is in an imposing old building filled with wood-paneled rooms. A typical court's calendar is jammed with many cases, and that day was no exception. The oral argument for my motion was not to take place for two hours, so I needed something to do. I decided to sit in the courtroom, get into my upright position, and just meditate.

As mentioned above, the three opposing attorneys were on average twice my age. They were all high-priced, experienced, and well-respected people who thought of themselves as powerful; they were used to pushing others around.

During my wait, I sat by myself in a corner of the courtroom and never moved a muscle. I did not even go to the bathroom. Although this incident happened a while ago, I will never forget it. I noticed that the three opposing attorneys were unable to sit still. They seemed anxious for the case to be called, and for the nasty business of eliminating my client's claim to be over. Meanwhile, I continued to sit there, literally doing nothing.

At one point, my eyes locked with those of Ned's attorney as he paced nervously in the courtroom. I returned the kind gesture he had made in his office; I stuck my index finger in my nose and pointed it directly at him. It was the only significant movement I made during the entire two-hour wait.

When the case was finally called for oral argument, Ned's attorney was required to present his case first, as he was the moving party in this motion. It was a fairly complicated case, and when he got up to speak, he mumbled incoherently, and confused the simplest facts. His disorientation was obvious to everyone. This appalling display from one of New York's most powerful litigators was mind-boggling. He had been a skilled and eloquent speaker on every prior occasion. Something was seriously wrong — but what?

The other attorneys and the judge looked at one another, struggling to find an explanation. This motion was supposed to provide a routine way for the other parties and the judge to be rid of my client and to greedily divide up the spoils. Nobody had anticipated this development. After three or four minutes of this embarrassing presentation, the judge interrupted Ned's attorney: "All counsel approach the bench." Puzzled and not knowing what to expect, I moved toward the judge along with the three other attorneys. The judge had barely acknowledged my existence before, but now she turned to me and asked, *"How much money do you want?"*

I was completely nonplussed, but I quickly recovered and made a fair six-figure demand. She accepted it on the spot and ordered a settlement based on that amount. This was the end of that case. The other attorneys were completely stunned and not exactly happy. On the way back to my seat, the judge's clerk rushed over to me and called me a genius. Even the other attorneys — except for Ned's — came over to congratulate me. They were in a state of disbelief.

Was I a genius? No. I didn't do a thing. I just sat there and never said a word. Was I even a great lawyer? I never liked the law and I was young, so I doubt it. Did I inadvertently tap into the energy that allowed me, as a novice, to bring down one of the most powerful attorneys in New York City? Absolutely! I'm sure you have experienced something like this before — a time when something great happened to you against all odds or prevailing logic, and you had no explanation for it.

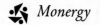

As I did, I'm sure you wondered, *What is going on here?* Can I ever reproduce these results? Is this some random magic, or are there rules that might apply? I set out on a journey to discover the answer. I didn't know it then, but I know now, that by not reacting and remaining calm, I allowed the full power of that lawyer's predatory energy to boomerang right back at him, rendering him incoherent. This instant karma effect is fully described in chapter 9. In that energy void, I also converted my opponents' negative energy into a financial bonanza for myself. Due to the intensity of the negative energy directed at me, my client's not-so-great claim prevailed.

It didn't matter that I never attended Harvard Law School, and it didn't matter that I was inexperienced and in my early twenties. The process of converting other people's negative energy into your financial gain is discussed at length in chapter 8.

This case was a huge epiphany for me, because I saw and felt first-hand that so-called powerful people could be brought to their knees by their own negative energy. My idea of what it means to be powerful in our society changed forever. Real power to create financial change is not about family background, the right schools, the right connections, or entrenched self-interest. It's not even about intelligence in the traditional sense. Power in every moneymaking situation is available to *anyone* who connects to the right energy and uses that energy responsibly. Learning how to recognize and access that energy is what this book is about.

Since that incident, I have further refined the energy concepts that apply to making money. Definite laws of energy apply to making and spending money wisely, and life is really about energy management.

If you apply those laws of energy with sincerity, miraculous results can become a more frequent part of your daily life, as they have for me.

Understanding my own and others' energy empowered me to exert control over my time, create the financial world I wanted, and change my life for the better. These are fast moving times with many electronic distractions. Even if you have lots of money, control over your time, maintaining peace of mind, and experiencing joy, can be elusive, and are the ultimate luxuries today. This book will help you reach these goals, too.

If you guess that I no longer practice law, you are correct. Why am I writing this book? As I look around at friends and loved ones and at the times we live in, I see increasing pressure on people to behave in selfish and self-destructive ways. Movies like *The Hunger Games* portray a society where survival of the individual comes at the expense of others' death. Bullying is on the rise, and not just in high schools; verbal bullying by the "haves" against the "have-nots" is tolerated more and more worldwide. Self-absorption is pervasive due in part to our celebrity-driven culture, and people's addiction to their smartphones to the exclusion of who and what is around them. This myopic energy is part of the way many people go about making money. Many people have no idea how their actions and energy affect others, and they seldom care.

Monergy is about creating more than enough money for your needs and wants. You can reach that goal if you apply this book's principles to develop your own prosperity consciousness while you tap into the energy to get what you really want in life. You will learn how to recognize, and transform other people's negative energy to your own financial benefit.

But this book goes beyond that. You will appreciate how everything you say and do creates energy. You will see how all energy in your personal and business lives is related, and you will respect this knowledge, because it can spare you from many of life's misfortunes. *Monergy* shows you how to create wealth while you benefit everyone you meet, and how to sustain wealth once it is created. Most of all, *Monergy* is about savoring the wealth you create.

A unique treasure exists in each of us. Understanding energy provides access to that creative gold. *Monergy* transports you to personal abundance in any economic cycle. It's your moment-to-moment choice to create the financial world you want through your consistent and sincere efforts to apply this book's principles. *It all starts with you.* The difference you can make in any situation is amazing.

- Energy controls every life process, including making money.
- The power to access money is available to everyone who taps into the right energy and uses it responsibly.
- You can identify and convert another person's negative energy for your own financial well-being.
- Understand the energy connection between your business and personal life.
- Create a positive energy exchange with everyone, and observe the effects on your wealth.

CHAPTER 2

ENERGY DETOX

You may have spent your whole life trying to make enough money, but not have achieved your goal. You may feel frustrated and want to do something about it. This chapter will show you why what you think — your attitudes, and what you do, your behavior — have been holding you back from obtaining wealth.

This chapter will:

- Shake you up by challenging entrenched beliefs.
- Make you aware, perhaps for the first time, that everything you think, say, and do is composed of energy.
- Show how your moneymaking energy cannot be contained, and how it impacts every part of your life.

It is unlikely that you can drop a lifetime of behavior in an instant. Learn to observe and recognize when certain attitudes and behaviors arise. Monitor how you feel when you refrain from any of these attitudes or behavior, and note whether your energy feels any different. Let's start with:

ATTITUDES
Other People's Money

Other people's money (OPM) — refers to an attitude, reinforced by just about every media outlet in Western society, that causes you to think too much about how much money other people have. This concern with what other people have has always existed, but it was heightened in the early 1980s when the media began focusing on lifestyles. It's hard not to get caught up in what other people have, especially when celebrities, or business billionaires, always seem to be in your face. And if you live in a major metropolitan area, you are surrounded by gaudy displays of wealth. The problem with OPM is that it doesn't matter whose money you're looking at since it's not your own. From an energy standpoint, concerning yourself with how much money anybody else has is one of the biggest mistakes you can make because you automatically denigrate your life energy. Money lust may be considered normal in our success-obsessed culture, but you can opt out of it once you realize it does not serve you well. In fact, it is one of the prime reasons you don't have what you want.

If you go to a cocktail party or any social gathering, you can readily see examples of this behavior. Someone will try to impress you with what they have accomplished, or with how much money they have made. Many of us encourage this type of conversation by nodding approvingly, or even by trying to beat these people at their own game. However, nobody wins by playing those games, and you only perpetuate false values.

For many people, concern with OPM is a priority. It seems that everyone wants more today, is eyeing what you have, or is clamoring to get things easily. And when perceptions shift in times of recession, people want to know who has lost the least. Concern for OPM is an avoidance technique. It is a waste of your precious life energy that would be better applied to improving your own situation.

In my early twenties, I fell victim to the grass-is-greener mentality and was seduced by OPM. When I graduated from law school and moved to New York City, I couldn't believe the high cost of an apartment that in any other place would be considered a joke. Since I had no special connections, I struggled to obtain an apartment and a job. My circle of friends included those from wealthier families who had some impressive toys. I was envious of their things, but I had no idea how those special frills affected their self-esteem.

My envy did not last long. As I've changed, so have they — but in fundamentally different ways. I've run into them over the years, and found many of them still searching for their own identities. Some appear burdened, not liberated by their money, and many seem old beyond their years. I attribute this to some seldom-acknowledged facts: struggling for what you have in life creates real character, reduces insecurity, and allows you to enjoy the earned proceeds. It's not a competition: it doesn't matter how much money anyone else has. It matters what you have, and it matters a great deal how you obtain it, and what that process means to you.

Reverence for Money

Reverence for money is a similar attitude to OPM, but it is more subtle, more pervasive, and automatically assumed to be true. It is communicated through the media, and the automatic admiration many have for those with a flashy life reinforces it.

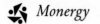

Celebrity worship feeds upon the reverence for money. It suggests that you are somehow inferior until you have a life full of the superficial trappings of the Kardashians, or at least aspire to owning those things. Everyday conversation demonstrates how reverence for money is pervasive. You can sense it in the way people talk about lots of money in hushed tones. It's as though money has some special power, and those who have it possess an innate superiority. But from an energy standpoint, reverence for money is flawed; it ignores the innate value that everyone possesses, and it often leads to unintended and undesirable results. Everyone wants enough money to fulfill their needs and dreams, but automatic reverence for those who possess large amounts of money is something to avoid.

I was exposed to this attitude while working as a lawyer for a real estate company. My boss spoke with an almost hypnotic reverence for his father, who preached that, "those with money called their own shots." Being curious, I asked him about his father's fate. His father had died of a stroke at the age of fifty-five. I could almost feel the pressure his father had placed on him to obtain lots of money.

Reverence for money can initiate life choices that go against your nature to obtain security, but you are playing with dangerous energy when you do this. Such choices are considered normal and acceptable in some circles, regardless of the price paid to get lots of money. The psychological and physical damage caused by an obligation to someone you don't really love is hard to calculate, but it may play a part in causing your body to self-destruct. Underneath the veneer of all that money, you begin to hate yourself for selling out. Most people assume that diseases, such as cancer, come out of nowhere and strike mysteriously. I believe that 99 percent of all illnesses, including cancer, are created by an imbalance of energy in the mind/body system.[1] That energy imbalance frequently starts on the emotional plane, where it cannot be seen or touched, but it is most certainly felt.

Circumstances lead most of us to seek our own money, rather than depend on handouts from others. In that moneymaking process, a huge advantage can be had by reducing our reverence for wealth, and by becoming more detached. Reverence is the opposite of detachment. Reverence for money is like desperation for love — an energy that repels the very object it seeks.

The notion of detachment comes from Eastern philosophy, and for many Americans it is an alien concept. Detachment does not mean not caring; it means not focusing so much on the end result, and allowing things the space and time to fully develop. Your ego and self-image become less wrapped up in your goal, and you become less needy. When you become more detached, you shift your focus from how everything affects you, to a more bemused observation of everything that happens around you. Through detachment, you create an energy sphere with more space, more freedom, and more flexibility; ideal conditions for your financial goals to take shape.

My choice to be detached helped save one of my first real estate investments. I went to contract on a small factory in Brooklyn that made halvah, a Middle Eastern candy. I still chuckle whenever I see halvah being sold in a store. This factory was on the periphery of a developing Brooklyn neighborhood, and I hoped to convert it to residential usage.

1. See my blog post on self-healing at http://www.monergylife.com/the-healing-process

I was just starting out in real estate investing, and obtaining the needed financing for this commercial building was difficult. Thus, I decided to assign, or sell, the contract before closing and to try to make some profit. This proved quite challenging.

I had additional pressure, too. I thought I was getting a good deal, so I agreed to two tough terms in the contract: I had to close by a certain date (time of the essence), and my contract was not conditioned on my getting financing. If I couldn't get financing (and it turned out I couldn't), and I didn't sell my contract before the closing date, I was going to lose my down-payment, which was a lot of money for me at the time.

I listed the property with quite a few real estate brokers, and one of the brokers found someone to buy the contract from me before closing, which meant I could flip it and preserve my down-payment. The timing was tight, because the sale of that contract was going to conclude two days before I needed to close on the original deal. Although I was inexperienced in the real estate business, I figured out two things: I needed to move fast, and I needed the best lawyer to represent me. I was lucky enough to find a real estate lawyer who was not only intelligent, but positive, helpful, and a pleasure to deal with — a rare find indeed.

I went to his Manhattan office on 57th street to sell my contract to this buyer, who would then close with the original seller two days later on the underlying contract. The deal proceeded smoothly for about two hours until the buyer made a demand I couldn't satisfy. My lawyer looked at me with a face that said it all: "Nice try, but it looks like this won't fly." I said nothing, excused myself from the conference room, and went to a window to survey the concrete landscape of midtown

Manhattan. I stood there for a few minutes, took some deep breaths, and returned to the meeting. It was 3:00 PM. I looked that buyer straight in the eye and said, "You know, I can't be bothered by this. I haven't eaten yet, and if you don't want to complete this, just let me know. I'll go to lunch right now."

My lawyer looked at me as though I was crazy, because he knew I had no one else to buy my contract. With barely one day left to find someone, it was unlikely I would get anyone else. Nevertheless, *I acted like I didn't need this buyer at all.*

It worked! The buyer suddenly dropped the demand that I could never satisfy, and bought the contract from me. Not only did I not lose my down-payment, but I made a small profit, too. When the transaction was completed and the buyer left, I spoke privately with my lawyer. He not only congratulated me, but refused any payment for his services. He even offered me a job with his law firm. I thanked him profusely, but I respectfully declined his offer. I had other plans — and besides, I still hadn't eaten lunch!

Experiment with detachment. You will find that the space and freedom you gain enhances any moneymaking opportunity — and it feels great, too.

Wanting Too Much Money

I know what it's like to have a stack of bills you can't pay, or to think twice before making a purchase, or taking a cab home. Of course, you want to be able to do more than pay your bills. You want to have enough money for things and experiences that just appeal to you, and to feel economically secure in tumultuous times. Having a lot of money can increase your range of choices, which is a great thing

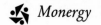

if handled responsibly, but some of those choices can be dangerous. Having lots of money can stir up unpleasant feelings in those around you, especially if the people in your circle are not as prosperous, are inclined to comparison, or are going through rough times. And if you choose to flaunt your money, do so at your own peril. Quiet enjoyment of whatever you have will never lead you astray. There's a great French expression from the *Fable of the Crickets: "Pour vivre heureux, vivans caches,"* which literally translated means "to live happy, live hidden."

Could you really ever have too much money? Are you smart enough to avoid the perils of wealth? Quite some time ago, Bill Cosby's son was targeted, stalked, and killed on a Los Angeles freeway while driving a hundred-thousand-dollar Mercedes. I doubt he would have attracted the same attention in a Honda. Remember JFK Junior's plane crash off Martha's Vineyard? It was an act of God and a tragedy of great magnitude, but a tragedy like that could only happen to someone who could afford to buy and pilot a private plane for a weekend getaway.

Tragedy is hardly reserved for the wealthy, but wealth opens up new ways to make yourself more visible, and a target of the envious and greedy. Think about how much money you need to achieve your goals and dreams, and how little you need to impress anyone who truly matters to you.

Money is a double-edged sword. When discussing money, most people only say, "I want more." Strive to be *intelligently* rich, and enjoy your money to the maximum. Think about these subtleties *now,* as you embark on your new moneymaking process.

BEHAVIOR
Manipulating Other People

What could possibly be wrong with manipulating other people? It's a dog-eat-dog-world, right? Not exactly. Contrary to what is depicted in television and movies, when you force or manipulate someone to do something they wouldn't do voluntarily, you rarely get the results you want. And even if you get the results for that moment, resentment is an energy that can linger, so try to avoid it. You don't have to become Mother Teresa, but even a small and gradual shift away from manipulative behavior reaps huge benefits: it changes the energy to a "get-rich" frequency.

One of my good friends is second in command of a foreign airline's New York office. He is quite fortunate, because as part of his job, he flies to all parts of the world to monitor the effectiveness of his directives. Of course, he has unlimited travel benefits, so he frequently flies to far off destinations just to enjoy a long weekend. He is very intelligent and usually quite well meaning.

He complained to me that his New York boss was completely incompetent, an alcoholic, and was cheating on his wife, too. I asked him how someone so filled with deficiencies became head of the New York office. He told me it was politics, plain and simple; his boss was imposed on him by the European headquarters. My friend hatched a plan to get his boss fired, and because he was so confident of his intelligence, he was sure he would succeed.

We didn't speak for some time, and when we finally had dinner, I asked him what had happened with his boss. He laughed for a few seconds but said nothing. I asked him again, and then he told me. He had succeeded in getting his boss fired, but his new boss was worse than the old one.

There is nothing wrong with wanting to improve your life's situation, but there is a huge energy difference between winning at any cost — often by manipulative means — and just plain winning. When you choose to win at any cost, the experience that follows will rarely be optimal.

Passive-Aggressive Energy

Passive-aggressive energy is epidemic in our politically correct world. We all engage in this behavior without thinking about it. When you promise to contact someone by phone, text, or e-mail and never do, the person you committed to is left wondering why. If you knew that this created bad energy that affected your life and your ability to make money, you would be more careful with your promises. *Following through on even the smallest promise affects other areas of your life because everything is an energy exchange.*

I was recently on the receiving end of passive-aggressive behavior I had done nothing to provoke. I had decided to renovate several properties I own in order to sell them. I hired two contractors for this project, both of whom failed to complete work in the promised timeframe. Neither of them offered any excuse for the delay. They knew that I planned to sell these properties, and that their passive-aggressive behavior interfered with that goal. They were not malicious, but they were casually indifferent.

I also hired a young designer to help renovate those properties. She was still in design school, and I sensed that this job was important to her.

She prepared a two-page contract that I signed promptly after making a few small changes. I made sure to pay her on time.

With that energy swirling around me, here's what I did: Because of the passive-aggressive behavior of the contractors, and my own positive-directed energy toward the young designer, my energy was clean, and I had an *energy advantage*.[2] Rather than yell at these contractors for their behavior, I looked for an opportunity to convert their negative energy to my benefit.

An opportunity arose soon when I spoke to a relative who worked for a major LA art collector. His employer had just bought fifteen large art pieces from a young Japanese artist, part of the Kaikai Kiki artists' collective. The total cost of these works was $300,000.

He explained the two-tiered system of art purchases. Galleries reserved the works of hot artists for serious art collectors only, which forced speculators or the general public to buy them at a premium when they were auctioned. I expressed interest in buying some of this hot Japanese artist's work if a chance arose.

The next day my relative called me because his employer didn't want one of the fifteen pieces allocated to her. I had one hour to decide if I wanted to buy it, so I quickly checked out the artist's work on the Internet. The available piece was an amazingly beautiful, strikingly original, twelve-foot long piece of art that I instantly decided to buy because of its great energy.

The price of the painting was not cheap, but it had the potential to be worth substantially more in the long term. This artist had recently created a fifty-foot lobby installation for the renovated

2. The concept of energy advantage is discussed at length in chapter 8: Converting Negative Energy to Money

Museum of the Moving Image in Astoria, Queens. This artist's mentor, Takashi Murakami, is world famous, and was named one of the top ten artists for this *millennium.* Most importantly, this painting added a new dimension of enjoyment to my life. I had a perfect spot for it in my Miami loft.

This opportunity came about because the building contractors who had promised to complete certain work for me hadn't done so on time, giving me the *energy advantage.* I let go of the idea that I had to punish them in some way or exact revenge, which would have caused me further harm and not created a financial benefit. Because energy is fluid, my conversion of that negative energy procured this unique piece of art, which promises to increase dramatically in value. More importantly, the painting is unique and beautiful, and I have enjoyed it over and over again.

Learn to see energy connections in every part of your life, and the importance of keeping even the smallest of your promises. The changes you make, and your increased awareness at every step, will open up experiences and opportunities you never could have imagined.

Legacies to Children (leaving money to your children)

Most parents naturally want the best for their children. We want all of their needs taken care of, and we want to give them a better life. But how much money is necessary, or even desirable, to bequeath them for this purpose?

I grew up in an adequate but by no means elaborate apartment in Queens, New York, where there was a real sense of community. I shared an eleven by thirteen-foot bedroom with my brother until I was fifteen, when we moved to a much larger and nicer apartment in which I had my own bedroom. I never did without the important things, but I didn't grow up in the lap of luxury. The schools were progressive and the crime rate was relatively low. I knew that my parents loved each other and that they loved me. My parents made the time to be there for my brother and me, but I also knew we had monetary constraints.

From an energy standpoint, it would be hard to offer a better upbringing. My parents were not saints, and I had some issues with them later on in life. However, we were fully aware of how lucky we were to have one another, and to witness the struggles and triumphs in our lives.

There is nothing wrong with sharing your success and achievements with your own children, *provided* it's accompanied by appropriate reality checks. Otherwise, you may be harming your kids. When it comes to leaving money to your offspring, less is probably more. It is the rare individual who appreciates anything presented on a silver platter, and money is far from the only valuable bequest available. The most powerful gift to children is to instill in them respect for self and for others, love of all life, true compassion, and preparedness for life as it actually is. Allow your children to struggle so they can feel their own strength and develop real character. Follow those suggestions first, and any money you leave them will be icing on the cake.

Playing the Lottery

What could be more innocent than playing the lottery? In a way, nothing — but it does little to make you rich, and it negatively affects your energy; it wrongly suggests that your fortune in life is random. A slogan

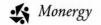

in commercials for the New York State lottery proclaims: "Hey, you never know." Well, I *do* know. The chances of anyone actually winning a large lottery are about the same as those of a postal worker being able to deactivate a nuclear bomb. I love to take chances, and if you don't take chances, you'll probably never get what you want in life, or feel truly alive. Take chances when the crucial energy components are present and properly aligned. Those instances offer a real possibility for building wealth. When you determine that a certain playing field is not promising, just walk away.

When you stand in line to play the lottery, you are buying into the fallacy that, "if I win those millions, then x, y, and z will occur; then I'll become happy and my life will automatically become so much better." That is not how your life is going to unfold, even in the unlikely event that you win. Instead, refuse to admit that you lack the power right now to tap into the energy around you to create what you want. To do otherwise is to devalue yourself — and to embrace bad energy.

Time Management

Your time on this planet is both non-renewable and precious. Avoid uncomfortable situations, and question old assumptions. Begin to see your life as one of choices, not obligations. If you feel you must be physically present in a situation, but are mentally dreading it, stay away. By seeing your life as one of choices, you bring a clearer and more positive energy to your commitments. As an experiment, consider seriously whether or not you must spend time with certain people or in certain situations. Do you notice a qualitative change to your energy? Do you feel freer to pursue what you really want?

Exposure to Media

In our digitally obsessed times, you can easily become overexposed to media, including phone apps, movies, the Internet, and video games. This exposure can make you passive or paranoid; it can seep dangerously into your consciousness as a substitute for reality, or take the place of actual experience. Addiction to social media, such as Facebook and Twitter, is only starting to be recognized as a problem. Too much of the wrong visual stimulation can also contribute to a more combative reference point for everyday existence, which may spawn outbreaks of senseless violence. On the other hand, some movies can be downright inspiring and a great vehicle for change — or just plain fun. YouTube has some funny videos, but how much of your time do you want to spend being distracted? When you do choose an on-screen form of entertainment, choose quality.

You can never go wrong with live activities, such as concerts, plays, museums, or just spending time with friends. Without the assault of moving pixels, you may discover hobbies that capture your attention. You might even decide to write a book! Not being bombarded by manipulative messages about your success allows you to thrash things out for yourself and have more genuine life experiences, such as taking a trip to somewhere totally new.

Your behavior, beliefs, and attitudes form the engine for your money-making efforts. Examine and then release the ineffectual elements that have prevented you from realizing your financial goals: other people's

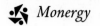

money, reverence for money, manipulating other people to get money, and wanting excess money.

You'll need to monitor your behavior closely to achieve this, but this cleansing is more than worth the effort. Your awareness of your own and others' passive-aggressive behavior will astound you, you will value your time as precious, you will re-think how much money is necessary for yourself and your family, and you will consider the effects of all electronic stimulation.

- It is disempowering to revere money or crave what others have (OPM). Focus on your own prosperity.
- Explore how detachment allows new opportunities to arise.
- Value experiences more than things.
- Avoid manipulative and passive-aggressive behavior.
- Don't leave so much money to your children that they no longer reap the benefits of life's struggles.
- See your life as one of choices, not obligations.
- Carefully monitor the electronic media you are exposed to.

Are you ready to take a trip outside your comfort zone? All you need to do is turn the page….

PART II

ENERGY OF CULTURE

Monergy

CHAPTER 3

LEAVE YOUR COMFORT ZONE

We live in a materialistic culture where things are increasingly valued more than people. This tendency seems to be getting worse. I'm sure you've heard the saying: "When you die, the one with the most toys wins." But when you die, you leave your toys behind.

The "comfort zone" is the goal of our materialistic culture. It is the place people rush to get to and stay in where an abundance of goods and creature comforts provides a certain type of security and a barrier to unpleasant aspects of life. You are encouraged to think up-market, and to obtain goods that reflect your social status, whether or not those goods are needed or enhance your life. The comfort zone is linked to false ideas about prosperity, and these ideas are routinely exported to other parts of the world. We receive mixed receptions from other countries that, on one hand, want to improve their economies, but on the other hand, don't want their cultures obliterated in the process.

Being in the comfort zone can be one of the biggest barriers to financial change. Even if people are forced to be less materialistic when they have less money, they yearn to return to these values when their fortunes improve, so exploring this issue remains important. Your comfort zone is something to be aware of as you start tapping into prosperity consciousness, because it would be a terrible waste to use this book's principles to further enslave yourself or others. Don't use

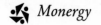

your increased wealth to insulate yourself in a harmful way, or for self-destructive activities.

Look around at the effects of the comfort zone. Too much emphasis on comfort can be harmful, particularly when more humanistic values do not prevail. It can have a numbing effect on teenagers and those vulnerable to superficial values. Even if we don't partake, we are all affected in some way by recreational drug abuse, alcoholism, and the increasing use of anti-depression and anti-anxiety medication. Many people need to counter the harsh nature of our culture — and much of that brutality comes from the mindless pursuit of money and the comfort zone. In that pursuit, "anything goes," and tragically, its effect on others is rarely considered. When a society values material things over the emotional needs of its people, it is more prone to senseless violence. This violence is often committed by emotionally starved people who crave attention, which accounts for many of the mass shootings that regularly occur in the United States.

Even those with lots of money may not get their emotional needs met because they are seeking more. I recently saw a young actress promoting her latest movie on a talk show. She earns at least ten million dollars a picture, and in a nod to her personal life, the host asked her about her mother's recent death. Her reaction was quite revealing, since she spoke of her mother's death and the need to go home as an inconvenient lapse in her movie's promotion schedule. You couldn't tell whether she had any real feelings for her mother, but in a sense it was irrelevant. It was clear that, in her mind at least, the importance of publicizing her picture took precedence over the time needed for natural grieving. I found it outrageous that her parent's death was so trivialized, and relegated to a position inferior to her professional pursuits. Even someone deemed important by society, like a celebrity, wasn't allowed sufficient time to grieve. On another level, she couldn't afford to grieve normally. How much additional money would she need before she could afford to do so? What does this say about the value our society places on the emotional needs of the general population?

The imbalance of our comfort zone mentality is especially revealed when a family's financial situation weakens. In a recent episode of a talk show, it was presented as a real sacrifice for a middle-class suburban family in the Midwest to go to the public library to rent videos, instead of paying for cable, or streaming movies at home.

This rush for more and more comfort produces many unintended effects that impact our psyches individually and collectively. Too much emphasis on comfort is, from an energy standpoint, an attempt to keep certain realities at bay. It can foster an "us versus them" mentality, and it creates a new class of people seduced by the appearance of things, rather than concerned with what's going on inside. Since the world is an increasingly small place where the struggles of humanity are displayed immediately and graphically in the media, a comfort zone mentality is a liability, especially when it creates an artificial insulation.

Getting outside of your comfort zone is a revelation. Several years ago, I took a trip to celebrate another moneymaking experience. I went to Southeast Asia and spent most of my time in third-world countries, such as Thailand and Vietnam. Although I stayed only in five-star hotels on this trip, I was firmly outside of the comfort zone. (The reasons I stayed in those hotels are explained in chapter 14). It was my first trip to Asia, but hopefully not my last. Almost every minute of every day was

a totally new and different experience. Just walking down the street in Bangkok was exotic. The sensory input was overwhelming due to the heat, pollution, and unbelievable beauty of the local sites.

People relate to one another on a totally different energy level in Thailand and Vietnam. Their behavior is infused with sincerity and modesty, a by-product of their Buddhist traditions. Most people in these countries are not living in the comfort zone, or in a life dominated by the media. People's lives in Thailand and Vietnam are real, and not stylized. Thus, your average interaction with people in these countries is going to be quite different from an encounter in the United States.

Prior to going to Vietnam, I had read a *New York Times* article about an artist in Hanoi who had designed propaganda posters during the Vietnam War. He had lived in an underground village for six years, and after the war, met with foreign visitors who came to Hanoi. This article piqued my interest because of my fascination with the Vietnam War. I thought this artist might have a unique perspective on the war. I had never been fully satisfied with the reasons for our involvement, or our loss in Vietnam, so I wanted to visit Vietnam and see what I could discover for myself. I had this article with me when I arrived in Hanoi on the last leg of my Asian journey.

Though I showed the article to the concierge at my Hanoi hotel (the Hanoi Hilton), he was unable to find the artist. Since it was early December, a Christmas party was taking place in the hotel lobby for the International School in Hanoi. I decided to have a glass of wine and mingle, so I conversed with those around me, including a young Vietnamese journalist covering the event for his English language newspaper. We talked about any number of things, including the artist I wanted to find. When I showed him the article from the

New York Times, he offered to locate the artist. He promised to call me the next day with the results of his inquiry.

The party for the International School soon disbanded, and the journalist invited me to go to a local jazz bar, which was a twenty-minute walk from the hotel. That was an interesting walk, since more than 90 percent of the intersections in Hanoi have no traffic lights or signs. The streets are wide with many traffic circles, particularly in the French quarter where I was staying. These traffic circles are filled with hundreds of motorbikes, bicycles, and cars going in every direction. As a pedestrian, you are advised to keep walking, regardless of the number of vehicles coming at you. If you stop or try to go back, you increase your chance of being hit. It amounted to a leap of faith, but miraculously, the system seemed to work.

The jazz club was fantastic. I engaged in fascinating conversations with both locals and expatriates, and listened to jazz performances by European and Asian artists. I said good night to my kind journalist friend, but didn't expect him to make the effort to find that artist. I was surprised when he called me the next day to tell me of his success. The person I was seeking was an artist in residence at the Fine Arts College of Hanoi, only a fifteen-minute taxi ride from my hotel. My journalist friend had already set up a meeting for me with the artist for later that day. I was beyond thrilled.

Meeting the artist was nothing like what I would have expected. I had learned to have no expectations and to take things slowly on this Asian trip. It was best to remain wide open to the experience and let events take their natural shape. I had difficulty finding the artist when I got to the Fine Arts College, because the artists in residence lived on a small side-street recessed from the main campus. It was he who found me walking behind the main college building looking lost. I guess there weren't too many six foot tall, sun-tanned Americans wandering around that school. The artist, a mild mannered man in his late fifties, seemed excited to meet me; he treated me as though I were a long-lost relative, or a celebrity. I was quite unprepared for such a warm-hearted treatment, as he was the well-known artist, and I was completely unknown to him. He took me to his door, we took off our shoes, and he ushered me inside a beautiful and elegant four-story townhouse.

He lived in that house for very little rent while he taught at the college. He took me on a tour of his art-filled house, but I didn't see any of the propaganda posters on the walls. We returned to the ground floor to have tea and get better acquainted.

We started to talk about the Vietnam War, and although his English was just passable, his son, who was also an artist and whose English was much better, soon joined us. His father had designed many of the propaganda posters used during and after the Vietnam War. The father confirmed that he had been an artist in residence during the Vietnam War, but not at any college. I learned that the North Vietnamese had created underground villages in areas that were subject to heavy American bombings — villages that are now popular tourist attractions.

The father told me that he had lived underground for six years during the Vietnam War. Take a moment to process that: six years underground! Imagine having to live that way for a day, let alone six years. Talk about the opposite of the comfort zone. There was absolutely no bitterness in his voice or demeanor, and he was unbelievably modest as he related the range of activities that existed in these underground villages. As I sat there in his house listening to his story, I had to admire this man and his life. He had a real life, not a lifestyle. And most amazing of all, he made no effort to portray himself as a victim for what life had brought him. The events of his life had made him stronger, more compassionate, and genuinely curious about other cultures. He showed me his pen-and-ink drawings of life in these underground villages, and I couldn't believe what I saw. There were underground screening rooms, theaters, schools, and housing. In fact, just about every activity you would typically find above ground was depicted, except that these functions were four and five levels below the earth in the middle of the Vietnam War.

During my three hours spent with father and son, they showed no bravado or made any attempt to rub the Vietnamese victory in my face. There was only the telling of a story with earnestness and sincerity. That level of sincerity is something I have rarely felt in the United States or anywhere else, but I felt it often in Vietnam — and not just with this artist.

The vast majority of Vietnamese were incredibly open and friendly to me, especially when they knew I was American. America unleashed incredible devastation on the people of Vietnam and its landscape. Although we lost approximately sixty thousand American lives, more than three million Vietnamese were killed, and exploding bombs caused horrible injuries for years after the war ended. It is common, even now, to see limbless people in the street who stepped on a mine in the wrong rice field. Nonetheless, almost all Vietnamese are trying to learn English, and they crave to know more about us. This exemplifies letting go and living in the present.

The artist told me with pride about his trip to Princeton University several years earlier to mount an art exhibition. I finally got around to asking him about those propaganda posters, which were not on display

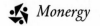

when he gave me a tour of his house. He went to a closet and took out a large portfolio, spread it out in front of me, and showed me about forty posters. They weren't propaganda posters in the way I had thought, because none of them dealt with Vietnam prevailing in the war against the United States. Instead, the posters were celebrations of different aspects of Vietnamese life, such as the importance of rice, the role of farmers, and the value of fishermen. They were original posters, copies of which had been plastered across Vietnam in a larger version. They spanned the years 1965–1985, because they also included posters from Vietnam's occupation/war with Cambodia that occurred after America left Vietnam in 1973.

I wasn't sure whether the posters were for sale, and I didn't want to offend my gracious host. Every poster was beautiful in a different way. As I pointed out the five posters that I particularly liked, he put them to the side. I purchased those posters with as much respect as possible, and felt honored that he would even sell them to me. These posters now hang in my New York apartment where they are a cherished remembrance. We took several pictures together in front of his house before I left, and he promised to send me copies. Coincidentally, the day after I started writing about this artist in this book, I received those photographs from him.

The artist's son hailed a cab and accompanied me back to my hotel. I asked him if he could give me receipts for the posters to avoid any trouble with customs. He told me that a friend of his owned an art gallery, and he would bring some receipts to my hotel the next morning. I didn't expect him to show up, because once people are paid in the United States they almost never follow up. But this was Vietnam where the acceptable code of behavior was to honor your word.

When he brought me the receipts the next day, he invited me for coffee at a local café. I welcomed the opportunity to find out even more about Vietnamese life, including additional input on the Vietnam War. He told me that contact with foreigners had opened up in the last several years. Not too long before, it would have been unacceptable for him to interact so freely with any foreigner, and he would have been too scared to have even met me in my hotel lobby.

I was still curious about the Vietnam War, so I kept steering the conversation back to that event. Of course, I couldn't help reaching my own conclusions after spending time in Southeast Asia. After almost three weeks, I could sense the futility of trying to dominate any of these local cultures. I mentioned the earnestness and sincerity of the people in Vietnam earlier. I also noticed a certain strength and pride in almost all of the Vietnamese I met, but this was a quiet strength that did not need to be hyped up. It just existed and you sensed it immediately. Although I have never been treated so graciously in any other country, I would not want these people as my enemies. The French and the Chinese also tried unsuccessfully to dominate the Vietnamese, but they are not of a character to be dominated by anyone. To understand the Vietnamese is to respect them as a nation, and to allow them to just be.

Vietnam has a very old culture with many rich traditions that I'm sure were never considered before we decided to get involved there. The energy of the people is different from what we are accustomed to, and their national consciousness is infused with a strong Buddhist tradition. When the Vietnamese culture was pitted against our kick-ass "America-is-great" comfort culture, the comfort culture lost.

I've heard friends, acquaintances, and media personalities say that the reason we didn't win the Vietnam War was that we never fought it at full throttle. I can only look at these people and shake my head. Some people imagine that the United States has not only the best culture, but a right and an obligation to impose it on others. It is sad that even after the debacle of the Vietnam War, more people don't question the idea of American cultural superiority. Third-world countries possess valuable cultural attributes that any open-minded American can learn and benefit from.

Remember the story in the first chapter about the powerful lawyer and his attitude of entitlement? How he was taken down by a novice he regarded as totally inferior, how he couldn't possibly understand that, and how vulnerable he became because he was so accustomed to wielding power over others? The United States in the early 1960s embodied many of these characteristics with its huge sense of entitlement and moral superiority. Throw in a large helping of ignorance, and history shows how we set ourselves up for a big fall, which is why we didn't win the Vietnam War. No quantity of extra bombs or troops or weapons could have altered the outcome; bombs don't destroy deeply held beliefs rooted in survival and national pride. In order to learn from that experience, we must identify and remember the energy dynamics of what occurred.

When I brought up the Vietnam War again with the artist's son over coffee at that café, it was interesting to hear his viewpoint. He had never viewed America as the enemy, although, being thirty years old, he had not fought in the Vietnam War. He viewed the Vietnam War as a continuum of other conflicts in which the Vietnamese have had to fight for national independence and freedom from foreign domination — and they have prevailed in that struggle over time. He also insisted that Ho Chi Minh, their most esteemed national leader, was not so much a communist as a nationalist. It is debatable whether that is true, but history shows that Ho Chi Minh was a sometime admirer of the United States Constitution, and he once approached President Truman for American assistance in ridding Vietnam of French colonial rule. His appeal was ignored by America, and he received a more sympathetic ear from communist China and the former Soviet Union, both of which possessed strong anti-colonial leanings, and were more than willing to fund the fight against America in Vietnam.

Young Vietnamese view America and capitalism as a vehicle for expanded personal liberty. Vietnam is now more open to foreigners and to limited forms of capitalism, but despite this thawing process, the Vietnamese strongly wish to preserve their national identity. I wish them sincere good luck.

Developments in Vietnam prove once again that you cannot force another person or country to take steps you want them to take if they are not ready to voluntarily make those changes. The idea that we as a country would know what is right for Vietnam is as presumptuous as an individual thinking he knows what's best for someone else — and acting on such an assumption makes a big mess. It comes down to a very simple energy principal discussed earlier: don't try to manipulate others to get what you want.

One of our goals in the Vietnam War was to keep Vietnam capitalist and prevent communism from spreading throughout Southeast Asia, the supposed "domino effect." This is now being accomplished voluntarily at its own pace and without war. Left alone and without any coercion, Vietnam is now embracing capitalism as more and more foreign entities establish business partnerships with them. In fact, it's rare to find a pair of sneakers in America that are *not* made in Vietnam, an ironic production source for the American comfort culture.

Before leaving Vietnam, I was fortunate enough to witness a meeting between representatives of a foreign corporation and two Vietnamese governmental officials. The meeting took place in the breakfast lounge of my hotel and was quite poignant to observe. The Vietnamese representatives were a young and freshly scrubbed man and woman who looked like they were right off the farm. I was close enough to observe their demeanor and hear their conversation. They seemed earnest and concerned with national interests, not just with consumerism. They had a certain refreshing naïvety about them — or to put it another way, they did not appear jaded. It was amusing to see the British representatives — somewhat overweight, and looking a bit jet lagged — try to convince the Vietnamese how the project would be beneficial to them. You could almost see the Britons counting the money they were going to make, while the Vietnamese were coming from a different place; their experience with corporate and business manipulations was just beginning.

History offers some strange lessons. As one of the last vestiges of communist rule experiments with capitalism, we in the United States may need protection from our own advanced form of capitalism, which is extremely innovative, but which has also assumed an alarming brutality. Just ask anyone who has gone on five interviews for a job and then not gotten it. The hypnotic reverence for money in our society keeps getting stronger for some, while others seek greater wealth parity.

My last evening in Vietnam proved a suitable end to a memorable visit. The Vietnamese journalist and a female friend met me at the hotel to take me to dinner. When I insisted it was going to be my treat, they asked me where I wanted to go. I told them I wanted to go somewhere with an historical ambience. They thought of the perfect restaurant in an old villa twenty minutes away by motorbike, and I immediately agreed.

Riding without a helmet on the back of a motorbike through the beauty of the French quarter, I felt transported to a different time and place — perhaps to the 1950s. I could appreciate Hanoi's lack of skyscrapers and its many older and distinguished buildings. I felt like a spy out of the post war era, a "Secret Agent Man." I also felt more than a little scared for my life, because as mentioned earlier, Hanoi has virtually no traffic control system. Cars, motorbikes, and bicycles were going in every which way. But isn't that part of the fun in leaving the comfort zone?

We arrived at the restaurant after a thrilling ride and were met by valet parking Vietnamese style — someone to take your motorbike and watch it until your return. The restaurant was a beautiful outdoor café in a distinguished old villa where the buffet encompassed virtually every kind of vegetable, noodle, meat, and fish dish you could want.

We spoke about a range of personal and political issues over the course of a two-hour dinner. We even discussed some of the ideas in this book, since it had not yet been written. It turns out that a lot of negative energy and manipulative people exist in the Vietnamese workplace, too. I didn't get the feeling that either of my Vietnamese friends was holding back. I didn't hold back either, and I felt free enough to joke around and even be a little sarcastic.

My Vietnamese friends evinced a curiosity and earnestness so genuine that it was impossible not to like them, or to be moved by their circumstances in life. The restraints of their society still existed, but those restrictions were being challenged as we spoke; it was a very opportune time to be there.

A card was slipped under my hotel door the next morning as I was packing to leave. The journalist's female friend who had come to dinner, and who also worked in my hotel had written it in English:

"Hi there funny mean New Yorker! This is my card, together with all the best wishes. It's great to know you. I really believe in what you said about ... well people and things."

The card ended with one of the sweetest thoughts ever directed my way:

"Sail safely through each day."

Although Israel is a totally different type of country, I found a similar sense of national purpose and strength when I visited there. Some readers may not see any connection between the two countries, but both Vietnam and Israel offer good examples of life outside the comfort zone.

In Israel, most people grow up with the constant threat of annihilation hanging over their heads, which comes from a revolving parade of enemies. Besides the requirement for universal military service, imagine what it was like to live in Israel during the Gulf War in the early 1990s: Israel's major cities were visited by long-term bombing campaigns courtesy of Iraq's Saddam Hussein. *That is life outside of the comfort zone.* Many people assume that living in these conditions is a horrible thing, and that the comfort of a typical American suburb is more desirable. But a funny thing happens to people who are constantly faced with crisis: they pull together and develop a real sense of national purpose. They end up living more in a dynamic moment-to-moment existence and less in an insulated world.

In fact, Israel is sometimes cited in surveys as containing the happiest people in the world, along with countries like Denmark, Norway, Sweden, Mexico, Panama, and Colombia. Interestingly enough, the United States is almost never listed among countries with the happiest people. It could be that America's polarized society, with large helpings of blame, victimization, and violence, puts a damper on collective happiness regardless of wealth or available opportunities.

In a way, the history of the Israeli people is similar to that of the Vietnamese. Both groups have a long tradition of fighting off attempts to dominate and oppress them. The Israelis also have a strong sense of national identity and pride that is seen in their people's faces. They are constantly exposed to the threats of destruction and violence, so there is incentive to appreciate every moment. They are never far from some of the worst aspects of human behavior, but while acknowledging that these forces exist, they continue to enjoy life's sweetness. Indeed, Tel Aviv is now a sophisticated city, and a world-class destination for those *just seeking fun*. This is no small feat in the Middle East, especially when you are surrounded by forces seeking your destruction.

Even if you don't reside in a hostile environment, or are not ejected from the comfort zone by a reduction in wealth, it might be advisable to voluntarily leave it — just so you don't get too comfortable. The fast-moving times we live in reward flexibility, and the ability to feel unthreatened in all kinds of situations. You can leave the comfort zone on a daily basis in simple ways — such as by not seeking the same experience twice, or by not surrounding yourself with the same stimuli or groups of people. It is a part of human nature to crave predictability and to attempt to repeat good experiences, but it's not always possible, and may work to your disadvantage. By getting out of your comfort zone, you take a more active and conscious role with everyone you meet and in everything you do, and you become less self-concerned. You start to appreciate every moment for all that it offers, and you become grateful for all your blessings.

I once tried a little experiment when I was still practicing law. I appeared in court on a settlement conference and was called in with opposing counsel to speak to the judge. The judge urged a particular settlement, and then instructed us to leave his chambers to discuss the case. When we returned to the judge's room, I deliberately sat to the judge's left, instead of to his right where I had sat before. My aim was to give the situation a different point of view, and this had the desired effect for me. I looked at that case, at the judge, and at my opponent differently because I actively chose to. My action had an unexpected impact on the other attorney. He became flustered and blurted out, "You're sitting in my chair."

Obviously, it wasn't *his* chair, but by sitting in that chair for only five minutes, the attorney had sunk into his comfort zone. I ejected him from his comfort zone by sitting in "his" chair, and he didn't like it. This attorney put so much importance on things staying the same, which showed how strong his level of attachment was. The case was eventually settled, but I learned an invaluable lesson that day: the slightest modification to your expected environment or experience can produce considerable anxiety.

The desire to reproduce familiar and comfortable experiences accounts for the popularity of chain hotels and fast food restaurants.

However, if you are seeking to recreate your financial world, you should not only avoid such standard experiences, but actively make every experience new. Conditioning yourself to change puts you ahead of others in times of economic challenges. New opportunities are often created by drastic upheaval, but you must be unperturbed enough to see and take advantage of them.

Getting out of your comfort zone can involve cultivating new types of friends, new ideas, new interests, and new ways of looking at almost everything. The emphasis is on new. Even a good situation or relationship may become stale if not allowed to evolve. Being too comfortable is also the reason many personal relationships don't work over time. People in failed relationships often say that they "grew in different directions," which, more often than not, means one person was growing, and the other person was stagnant, felt threatened, or tried to cling or keep the other person back.

People naturally want to keep the ones they love in a comfort zone, protected and out of danger. But this can be a bad tendency when motivated by fear. Fear can make you vulnerable to other unpleasant and unfortunate events, since when you anticipate something bad happening, it often does. Fear takes you out of the moment, causes you to project way too far, and misdirects attention that could have been used to prevent a calamity in the first place. Most importantly, fear is the energy opposite of love, which is undeniably the most powerful force in the universe.

Too much time spent in your comfort zone fosters a consciousness of designated winners and losers, and officially sanctioned groups of people to hate and fear. In reality *there is only us*. Recognizing that we're all in the same boat, and that on a universal level we are all "one," is hard for some to do because it becomes impossible to feel superior to anyone. I received a valuable lesson in this when I entered the real estate business and began looking at properties in changing areas of Brooklyn.

I obtained the address of an available building from a real estate broker, and then drove by to inspect it. I had preconceived ideas about the people who lived in these areas, but my ideas were shattered when I encountered some of the nicest and most hospitable people ever. I wanted to see what a typical apartment looked like, so I asked a tenant I met in the hallway if I could see her apartment. Remarkably, that tenant allowed me to see her unit. She even guessed that I was interested in buying the building, and urged me to do it!

The tendency to stay in one's comfort zone can start early. Consider some parents' efforts to place their child in the right pre-school. Many people see this as getting on an Ivy League track early, assumed to be a good thing leading to money, success, and the comfort zone. Few parents see the limitations this may impose, and they don't gauge the effect of putting such competitive pressure on children so young.

There are other benefits to spending more time out of your comfort zone. You can feel free enough to switch your focus away from your smartphone, and actually notice who and what is around you. You can be more available to meet other people's emotional needs, and become less busy with unimportant striving. You can actually be there for someone when they need you. Who knows? You may prevent a huge catastrophe by talking to the disgruntled teenager down the block who was planning a shoot-out at his school. In addition to helping others, by not being so busy chasing money and the illusions associated with it, you notice opportunities that were previously obscured.

As you experience more and more time out of your comfort zone, you begin to appreciate what it really means to have it all. This is quite distinct from the media's concept of *having it all*, which usually connotes the self-involved pursuit of whatever you want, whenever you want it, with no concern about using and then disposing of anyone in your quest. Forget about having it all for more than an instant, since sustaining what you have is never addressed. And those who promote having it all never think about the distress it causes people when they can't have it all.

The idea of having it all seduces many people. The notion of having the perfect job, house, and mate at the same time is appealing. Unfortunately it's a myth. Life unfolds at its own pace and presents you with opportunities when it wants to, not necessarily when it fits your agenda. By spending more time out of your comfort zone and by using the other principles in this book, your energy becomes more attuned to your environment. You embrace all that is happening now in a way that helps you and all those you encounter — a true "win-win" situation.

To remove yourself from your comfort zone, travel as often as possible to places that give you a unique perspective. Have experiences that require you to make adjustments. Don't be so impressed with the external appearance of things, like expensive new cars, fancy condominiums, or the people ensconced in them.

When I spent a long weekend in Medellin, Colombia (which I believe qualifies as *outside the comfort zone*), I rode in a funicular, part of an ambitious urban renewal program that goes straight through a *favela*, or slum. I walked through city squares teeming with people just hanging out in the middle of the day, and I felt a part of the universal energy in a third-world country. It was fascinating to observe how Medellin has moved on from being terrorized by Pablo Escobar. I highly recommend a trip there because it is not just off-the-beaten path, but is an eye-opening glimpse into humanity.

The comfort zone is seductive because it promises access to the latest gadgets, the most alluring residences and cars, and other related trappings. The problem arises when that is all you crave. If you want to increase your wealth, this addiction is harmful. You must leave the comfort zone and enter risk mode to make any meaningful financial shift.

- Honestly identify your comfort zone.
- Redefine its boundaries on a daily basis (i.e. try a new sport, food, or route home).
- Follow through on your commitments.
- View things from a neutral perspective without judgment.
- Plan a trip to somewhere unexpected.
- Watch new opportunities unfold.

CHAPTER 4

ABANDON SELF-ABSORPTION

Why do you need to understand self-absorption? What possible effect could it have on reshaping your financial world? The answer is *plenty*. As you begin your new money making process, it is important to remember that it's not all about you.

People have always been selfish, but this behavior has never before been displayed so openly without shame. This has been a gradual shift in our culture, accelerated by reality television and celebrity worship. A huge sense of entitlement has spread to the general population, and it now constitutes a value you are likely to encounter. Self-absorption manifests itself in the tendency to make a victim out of everyone. It is culturally accepted, when things don't go exactly the way one wants, to pass the blame to others. Lawyers are only too happy to exploit this tendency; they clog the courts with lawsuits for all sorts of victims, only some of whom have meritorious claims. Our tendency toward self-absorption accelerated in the 1960s when the phrase "doing your own thing" arose. That concept enabled people to explore unconventional values and ways of living — a very good thing. The downside of that freedom seeped into our national consciousness as self-absorption. People now justify almost any kind of behavior by saying: "I'm just doing my own thing." Fifty years ago, Andy Warhol identified the craving for "15 minutes of fame." He never anticipated it would become a lifelong endeavor through technology (Facebook, Smartphones, and Instagram)[3] creating a voyeuristic population seeking constant validation — self-absorption to the nth degree.

These cultural shifts affect your ability to reach your financial goals because no one operates in a vacuum. You live and work in a playing field that is filled with potential pitfalls, and which has been tilted by the media, changing expectations, and everyday behavior. As you start on one of the most challenging journeys ever — which is to create and sustain the financial world you want — you'd better not sabotage your goals. Identify your self-absorption and take steps to eradicate it. Spend less time thinking about yourself. Take responsibility for all of your actions. Own these actions, even if the consequences are not to your liking.

Self-absorption affects every part of society. I read an interview with a doctor who lived in a wealthy Ohio suburb, who was asked how the potential repeal of certain tax cuts would affect him. The doctor was married, in his late thirties, and he had five children aged one month through six years. His income was $300,000 per year, he lived in an $800,000 house with a pool, and his wife stayed at home with a full-time nanny. The doctor complained that his income was not high enough to comfortably afford college for all of his children. He defined "comfortably afford" as paying for all of his children's college education, with his children contributing zero.

The doctor argued that he deserved the proposed tax cuts, because when he became a doctor he assumed he would never have to worry about money again. The doctor claimed he needed a larger house to accommodate his sixth child, and would have to struggle to afford it.

3. The same technology has united the world and brought other enormous benefits.

He spoke with envy about people who lived in really rich neighborhoods. Entitlement reaches every segment of society.

It was appalling to read about this doctor who complained about his fate in life, given his age, income, and standard of living. In another time, not too long ago, a professional making so much money would have been reluctant to portray himself as one of society's victims. Not true today. And his attitude was even more objectionable given the economic challenges so many people face in paying college tuition for just one child (or in just feeding themselves).

The disease of self-absorption shows up in small but significant ways: a friend decided to bolt while helping me bring home those five Vietnamese posters from the framing shop because he wanted to look at ski equipment. Another friend claimed that a prized meditation tape I lent her before my Asia trip was a gift. She took four weeks to return it — complaining all the way. Self-absorption has become acceptable behavior, and hardly anyone questions it.

You don't have to live only to satisfy other people's needs. Enjoy your life; just try hard not to be self-absorbed. You can be one of the world's most free-spirited persons, and also one of the most responsible. The two can coexist, although most people seem to excel at one or the other.

We often label free-spirited people as "unstable" and responsible types as "boring." Those labels break down upon closer examination as both types engage in self-absorbed behavior. Be responsible in a genuine sense, not by just going through the motions. Don't ask anyone to take care of things you should be doing yourself. Try not to make gratuitous promises. If you say you will do something, make sure people can count on you.

You need not like excessive details or paperwork, or bureaucracies that exist solely to perpetuate themselves or stand in the way of progress. Don't be automatically impressed with professionals, or persons with multiple degrees. Learn to trust your own judgment over that of many professionals; yours is probably better intentioned, even when you have less technical expertise or education.

Take every opportunity to spend time in beautiful surroundings doing new things with as few distractions as possible. Rarely, if ever, let people hear you complain, as there is so much to be grateful for. Travel, eat great food, and make love as much as possible. These things are essential to the joy of living. They also boost your immune system and maintain your physical and emotional health.

Maintain a healthy dose of empathy for everyone you encounter, because life can be fragile. Regardless of someone's fate, never treat them like a victim, because doing so would only hurt, and not help. Make every effort to fulfill other people's needs and make their dreams come true.

These efforts make you less self-absorbed and also get you out of the comfort zone. It's rare for people to reach out like that today, and those who do are often viewed with suspicion. People are so conditioned to look out for themselves that time spent helping others is sometimes viewed as a waste. The truth is more nuanced. While you don't want to be used by others, offering help without expectation of payback and with a pure heart can never lead you astray.

Helping other people can be accomplished through something as simple as sharing information, or by doing a favor when asked, and not just when it is convenient. Information belongs to those who can use it, so freely share the information you have. There is no need to jealously guard your knowledge. Acknowledge a basic truth when you share information — that the information does not belong to you, but it has been revealed to you for a purpose. When you give it up, you make room for the information you need, too, so everyone gains and nobody stagnates.

Imagine a world in which you didn't encounter one complaining person during your day, a development sure to make you feel better. On a more modest scale, assume that one person reading this book changes their energy, stops complaining, and devotes their energy to reshaping finances while helping others along the way. Everyone in that person's sphere is impacted by that energy shift, and sometimes the benefits are enormous. How many people can one person meet in one year — a thousand people or more? *One person's energy makes a huge difference in this world.*

Self-absorption is the opposite of generosity — generosity of spirit, generosity of place, and generosity toward others. It produces energy counter-productive to the creation and sustenance of financial change. Misguided self-interest produces unpleasantness in the workplace, and it is a characteristic of the many sniveling, backstabbing, and brown-nosing types you have occasion to work with. Spend your time where that type of energy does not dominate, and create unlimited financial access for yourself.

It was never all about you. Wanting to improve your finances is a laudable goal, as long as you maintain awareness during the process. Self-absorption is an unfortunate by-product of basic human nature coupled with changes in our society that encourage selfishness and narcissism. It goes against an emerging world consciousness of "oneness" that suggests that there is one spiritual entity in the universe, that everyone and everything is part of this whole, and that what you perceive as physical separation is an illusion. You don't have to embrace this concept to acknowledge your own self-absorption and realize its harmful effects.

- Recognize self-absorption in yourself and others.
- Take full responsibility for your actions.
- Encourage everyone's prosperity and well-being.
- Make fewer promises but honor them all.
- Share your knowledge and time freely.

PART III

NEW ENERGY PATTERNS

CHAPTER 5

PROSPERITY CONSCIOUSNESS

Prosperity consciousness" is a mindset, a way of looking at life that creates abundance for you and those you encounter. At a young age, I intuitively sensed that a prosperity consciousness existed and was worth developing. However, those I knew believed and acted differently. When I entered the workforce and was forced to fend for myself, I was shocked at the things people said and did to get money. I kept raising this issue with those around me, but more often than not, I was rebuffed with comments such as, "That's the way it's always been," or "There's your business life and there's your personal life, and you can and should behave differently in each."

Something about this attitude didn't sit well with me. I was not about to put my head in the sand, endure years of unpleasant work, and then come up for a breather when I retired. I definitely believed that we were not put on earth to remain in a joyless and unrewarding situation, whether at work or in our personal lives. It may be a struggle to get to a better place, but I was willing to make the required effort. Besides, I never bought into the notion that you could behave like a monster in business without consequence, as long as you were a "nice person" in the rest of your life. As I began to observe behavior in the workplace, I found the opposite was true: there is no impunity for one's actions — anywhere, anytime.

I always had a strong sense that the legal field was not for me. Although I couldn't articulate why at the time, I can now: *It's all about energy.* There are many reasons why lawyers are disliked in our society. Lawyers often display unabashed arrogance, are trained to be nitpicking, and engage in contentious behavior to twist the truth. A courtroom perfectly showcases a system that fosters abuse: Judges and courtroom clerks insult lawyers and clients alike, suspend an individual's First Amendment rights, and get away with it. Many lawyers consider this normal behavior or don't want to jeopardize their livelihood by objecting too strenuously, so the status quo continues.

I also realized that I didn't want to spend my life under mounds of paperwork and fluorescent lights sorting out other people's mistakes. My life energy was too precious to waste in such a toxic environment. I needed a plan to get out. I appreciate now how lucky I was. I never let illusory power or phony privileges stop me from seeking a healthier venue, or being true to myself or happy. Many people use their money and position not for real enjoyment, but to have control over others, or for ego gratification. Remember Ned's lawyer in chapter 1 who was forced to give my client a fair piece of the estate? He's a perfect example of the kind of respected professional who, once you get past his smooth veneer and supposed status, is capable of all kinds of malice to protect his position and feed his ego.

A prosperity consciousness is what I was searching for. Once it is developed, you take control of your financial life, and dissolve any entrenched or powerful force blocking your goals. You may never encounter any one individual who can show you how to develop a prosperity consciousness, but by observing other people's behavior, you learn valuable lessons on how not to behave and think. You learn the importance of using whatever is around you, and of not bemoaning what you don't see or have. Ask yourself what's available right now, today, for you to work with. If you make gratitude an intrinsic part of this process, you're on the road to becoming a truly powerful person.

Know what is important to you financially, so you can put your new wealth together like building blocks. Set lofty goals for yourself as you appreciate the particular skills you have. Be determined to not let anyone control your life. Most people, if given a choice between actions that give them more money or power, or actions that result in your welfare, choose the path to money or control, so you must remain constantly vigilant. Don't worry; this awareness becomes second nature over time.

I made two very important promises to myself as I developed a prosperity consciousness:

1. If I reached my financial goals, I would avoid pushing others around. I would simply enjoy the money I earned to the fullest.

2. I would never merge with my money, meaning that neither my identity nor my appearance would be obviously tied to my financial status.

I have kept both these promises. You may want to make the same promises to yourself, or choose goals that appeal to you.

The Reciprocal Effect

Criticizing oneself in front of others is an amazingly common practice, yet it serves no purpose. *Stop doing it right now.* Forgive yourself for any transgressions you think you made, and forgive others for what you think they did to you. It will end the public self-lashings. Putting yourself down has nothing to do with being modest; it identifies you as a potential victim who is eager to be controlled by others. People will — on their own initiative — try to put you down and hold you back at every stage of any moneymaking process, so don't add to this fire. The corollary is also true. Do your best not to put others down. You are not entitled to any better treatment than you give other people.

Avoiding self-criticism and denigration of others are crucial first steps to realign your energy that demonstrate that you have fundamental appreciation for your own and others' worth. Even if another's effort falls short of your expectations, accept it as the best that person can make. When you give absolute respect to everyone, you will *get* absolute respect — this is the so-called "mirror effect."

By understanding the reciprocal effect — you'll be one step closer to making money with as little friction as possible. Isaac Newton said, "to every action, there is an equal and opposite reaction." This works on the emotional and spiritual planes as much as it does in the physical world. Consider all your thoughts and deeds in terms of the equal and opposite reactions they will produce. Positive actions taken on behalf of others produce benefits for you.

Develop Your Strengths

Get in touch with your true individual strengths, not the things you have been conditioned to pursue. Let your imagination and spirit run free. Remember that photography course you always wanted to take because you love photography so much? Remember those credits you needed to obtain your college degree so you could qualify for your dream job? Remember the satisfaction you got as a kid from working with your hands? This is the time to experience the things you really love, and to move away from the things you don't. You may not know where your true strength lies yet, but it will unfold as you try things that are linked to your passion and imagination.

Your everyday behavior may change as you explore, so don't be surprised at how people react to your energy shift. You will get comments from people that "something has changed," but they can't put their finger on what it is. You may find you are spending more time with different people, or are frequently alone. Don't be alarmed at any of this.

The people who will be most supportive of your efforts may be those you would least expect. Your close friends and family could feel threatened by your explorations, or they may be more comfortable with an unhappier you, since that person is who they know, and can control. Accept these fluctuations with an open heart.

Your efforts to identify your strengths cause new people, new experiences, and new opportunities to come out of the woodwork because your basic operating system is now tuned to a different frequency.

In my own case, I found the energy in the legal field repugnant and I wanted out. Once I honestly looked at my situation and tried new things, a strange and wonderful transformation began — proof that skills powered by passion cause contentment and prosperity.

Expand Your World

I started to choose things that felt right for me, rather than things I thought I should do. I got off my pre-programmed course. I decided to take acting classes at night, because those classes had a totally different energy than what I found in legal work. I had always wanted to act, but my serious professional career path discouraged it. Acting was the opposite of law in so many ways. Law was serious, problem-laden, and required constant deception. Acting was about having fun, being truthful, and living in the moment.

Some people say that being an actor and a lawyer require similar talent, but I don't agree. Both put on a show, but lawyers are trained to manipulate the truth; acting is about getting in touch with the truth in each moment, and reacting honestly.

Acting gave me entry into an entirely different world. It helped redefine my strengths and shift my perspective, which helped me to exit the legal field. After taking this one step and seeing that the world didn't collapse, I realized there were a lot more unexplored parts to myself than I had ever dreamed of. I went on auditions and worked as an actor in commercials, film, and television. I even worked on a music video in which a famous rock singer thanked me for my participation with a humility I will never forget. These acting experiences meant so much to me. For the first time, I saw that work could involve pure fun. I worked with people who loved what they did, and I witnessed a camaraderie I hadn't seen elsewhere — certainly not in the legal field where you are expected to destroy those who don't share your agenda. Since acting jobs are hard to obtain, I also witnessed widespread gratitude, something else I had never associated with work.

One of the best parts about acting is learning how to live in the moment, a notion that was completely foreign to me at the time. I now understand why so many people clamor to get into the film industry, despite all of its difficulties. Acting showed me that I could break away, try something new, and actually do it. It facilitated other shifts in my life, such as switching to the real estate business. Little by little, I started to see, believe, and internalize the notion that my life could change in fundamental ways.

Expand your world in traditional and non-traditional ways. Trust your gut feelings and start by exploring. Try new clothes, new activities, new places, and new people. Follow the roads that inspire you.

Ride the Waves

I opened myself up to a purer and more fluid energy, the type that makes everything happen. This energy is especially important in developing a prosperity consciousness. I call it *riding the waves.* With a goal in mind, along with conscious and pure energy, allow life to take you where it will; it could be anywhere. Another metaphor might be a *combustible stew* — you allow your pure and directed energy to mix with everybody's energy to form *who knows what?* Or you could call it a *great leap into the unknown,* where your best efforts are combined with those of others in the vast unknown, with the potential to create something magical. That is part of the pleasure and fun of this process, as you never know exactly what it will all add up to. In a sense, every creative project, including the process of making money, involves a combination of these elements.

Begin to view your life, including all of its components, as a work in process limited only by your imagination. Absolutely nothing in life is fixed, despite what some people would like you to believe. These beliefs are especially relevant to the flow of money, because once you see that things are in flux for everyone, you can reposition your mind and heart on the receiving end of life's riches.

Around the time I started acting, I picked up little hints and signals in other areas of my life. I allowed myself to admit that I had a feel for — or some kind of attraction to — buildings. The transition into real estate investing was a huge step for me, even though I was already a real estate attorney. It involved letting go of accumulated fears and recognizing a true interest in something other than the law. Also, the meaningless status of being a "lawyer" held too much sway with me. However, I was starting to feel differently about things, and was willing to take chances and look at things through a new prism. Practicing law never satisfied my soul, in spite of all my efforts.

I slowly put my foot in the water on the "other side" and a strange thing happened: buildings would actually talk to me. I don't mean they would say, "Hello. How's your day, dude?" I just somehow knew whether buildings were ripe for purchase and rehabilitation. I must have been crazy to buy the first property I bought because there were many unknown factors. It was a small apartment house in a somewhat marginal area of Brooklyn, subject to New York City Rent Regulations. It had been severely neglected, abandoned by its owner, and was being foreclosed on by a bank. I had been negotiating with that same bank on behalf of a client to purchase two other buildings when I came across this building, and got a brilliant idea — *why don't I buy it for myself?* I had always wondered what being a landlord would be like, but apprehension had always stopped me. It didn't this time. I had to scrape together every resource I could muster, but doors opened from the most unlikely sources, and I did it. This initial purchase opened a portal to the other side, and the experiences that followed were a roller coaster ride that fulfilled my dreams, and so much more.

Landlord-tenant relations in New York City are often perilous. Landlords typically despise their tenants, and vice-versa. I wanted to avoid that kind of energy in my properties, particularly in this first building. I laugh so hard when I think about this: For the first few years of my ownership, we gave out flowers on Mother's Day (to all the mothers, of course). This was a small gesture, and I think it was a rare one, too, because when I told this story to other landlords, they just scratched their heads or made fun of me. But when a problem developed at that building, such as the boiler going down in a cold snap, those tenants never rushed to crucify me or haul me into court, a common fate for many New York landlords. Also, I was never forced to go to court to collect rent from any tenant, because I worked out rent issues without court intervention. That first building led to other opportunities in New York real estate; each one had its own learning curve and cast of interesting characters.

Ride the waves in your life by following impulses, hunches, or long-standing wishes. Dedicate yourself to finding opportunity, and if and when fear arises, don't react; watch that fear dissolve into the nothingness from which it came.

Take Risks Alone

By "take risks alone," I don't mean you need to do it all on your own, because nobody can do that; we all need to work with other people in this world. But when it comes to the risk part, the stepping into the unknown, it is best to experience as much of it alone. Otherwise, you never really feel the power and sheer exhilaration of that energy. It remains an abstraction rather than an actual experience you can feel, refer to, and repeat. The rewards are also reduced if every time you take a chance, you have to tweet about it, or post it on Facebook for all your friends to see.

Taking risks on your own does not contradict what psychologists say are the benefits of expressing yourself and not keeping things inside; you should communicate with those who are a part of any project. But refrain from discussing your activities with those outside your inner circle. Gratuitous talking will only dilute the energy you need to reach your goal.

If you share your risks unnecessarily before your goals manifest, you will be subject to probing questions from others: "How is that thing going?" These questions that monitor your progress take focus away from the importance of the process itself. You end up looking for approval, or playing for an audience, rather than taking the necessary and sometimes difficult steps required to reach your goal.

I once made a limited investment in the stock market. I decided to talk about it with two people close to me. Talking about something as I'm doing it and while I'm in the risk zone is something I almost never do, but I wanted to see how talking about this stock might affect its performance. The stock I purchased had reached a high of more than fifty dollars two years before this purchase, and was at that time trading for less than one dollar. In fact, the stock had been driven down to twenty-five cents. I thought it was unfairly beaten down, so I bought a large number of shares. This stock appealed to me intuitively, although I don't claim to know a lot about the stock market.

Several years before that purchase, I met a few people who worked for this company, and I admired their intelligence. I couldn't imagine they would let this company go under. At the time I bought this stock, the overall stock market had sustained considerable losses, and had no discernible direction. Two months after I purchased it, the stock went up to sixty-five cents — a 150 percent gain.

I then told two people very close to me about the stock, and they subsequently bought it. They kept talking to me about the stock, and these conversations were filled with a high dosage of their nervous energy. When I witnessed how anxiously they were monitoring the progress of that stock, I knew it had been a mistake to tell them about it. I felt that the natural flow of that stock was being strangled, and I was right. The stock soon went down and was trading in the forty-three to fifty-cent range, when I sold it. My initial goal for this small investment had been to ride the stock up to one dollar, then hope it started to trade in dollar increments, rather than cents. Even though I still made a large return on this relatively small investment, I frustrated my goal of riding this investment all the way up. However, it reinforced a very valuable lesson: Do not talk about things while they are happening.

At the same time I made this stock investment, I refinanced two of my properties to take advantage of low interest rates. If completed, the refinancing of these two properties would provide a huge financial benefit to me. I made sure to not tell a soul what I was doing, and I focused solely on getting it done. The refinancing went seamlessly.

Other benefits accrue when you take more risks alone. Your fate will gradually change because you have stopped putting your financial future in the hands of anyone else but yourself. You have stopped playing the lottery with millions of other people. As you become more comfortable with taking risks, you go one-on-one with the gods, and as they dangle you over the precipice, dangle them right back with even more joy in your heart. The more you enter the risk zone alone, the more the gods love and reward you — because you demonstrate your faith, not fear, when confronted by the unknown. As you get more involved in this process, you can't help but develop enormous respect for the powers you are tapping into. These powers should not be taken lightly, and should never be claimed as yours, or as belonging to anybody.

You become privileged in its true sense, as opposed to the way most people define "privileged," as denoting great wealth or status. You get to access the core energy that really makes things happen as you make your financial goals a reality. Instead of being controlled by others, you take steps to actively control your destiny. *This is arguably the highest and best use of free will you will ever find.*

I have been accused of being mysterious or secretive, even by those close to me. I respond by saying, "Ask me anything." Friends have been surprised to learn of projects years after they occurred. They ask, "Why didn't you talk about them sooner?" But my goal was never to withhold information or to impress anyone with what I was doing. My goal was to stay focused and not dilute the energy of success.

In these voyeuristic times, I understand why people feel entitled to know everything. Many people are connected electronically all the time and rarely spend any time truly alone. Everything is documented for all to see. Being alone has become something feared and/or misunderstood. People need to keep talking on their cell phones no matter what they are doing, just so they won't be "alone." Even if being alone is not feared, it is certainly not encouraged, which is a shame. Quiet time allows ideas to emerge from the source and give your life direction.

There are other important reasons why you should take risks alone. If you think of your access to energy as coming from a type of pipeline, it is hard work to open up and sustain that pipeline to financial change. You want the pipeline to be as direct as possible, without breaks or detours. By taking risks alone, your energy is where it belongs — focused, strong, and working for you to achieve your financial goal.

An unintended but priceless side-effect of your efforts is that you grasp the value of *aloneness,* and its distinction from *loneliness.*

Money as By-product

In developing and sustaining a prosperity consciousness, think of money as a by-product of doing the right thing, rather than as a goal in and of itself. Many people walk around saying or thinking they want to be rich, or want to have x amount of dollars. They have no particular plan on how to make that money, nor are they concerned about the effects of their get-rich efforts on other people. From an energy standpoint, that type of attitude is unnecessary and counterproductive. How you make money is important, and what you do with that money is just as crucial.

I held onto my legal profession too long, thinking it was practical. I was afraid to make the necessary changes to get out. I only wish I had listened to my inner voice sooner. It's no coincidence that every position I ever had in the legal field never gave me *enough* — of anything, because it was the wrong field for me. Whenever you find yourself pushing something too hard, it's probably not for you and it will have a short shelf life. Consider moving on.

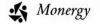

Once I let go of the things that weren't working and spent more time on the things that I loved, my world opened up, and I soon had more money than I had ever dreamed of. The money coming into my hands was a by-product of my doing what I was supposed to do, but it wasn't the prime objective. Doing the things I loved every day was payback enough. I couldn't believe how lucky I was to be just trying these things. I had no guarantee that I would succeed in the traditional sense, but I didn't care. The fact that I was no longer hitting walls in my life made my level of satisfaction skyrocket. I started to experience life as an adventure, and I was enjoying the ride. I found every day and almost every endeavor to be the creative act it is supposed to be.

I saw the process that went into each of my experiences, and I could repeat that process. I had identified and tapped into a particular energy — like logging onto the Internet. I was living in prosperity consciousness every moment. If you are wondering how long the process of tapping into your own prosperity consciousness takes, there is no set time. In a sense, it takes a lifetime commitment to an entirely new process, but some of the changes you will see are immediate. The best part of all this is how inspired you start to feel.

Sustain Your Prosperity

This is not your typical self-help book on how to become rich. I hope it puts the moneymaking process in a new light. Thus, it is important to discuss the skills required to sustain prosperity once you've got that flow going and are reaping the desired financial benefits.

Some of us have been conditioned to "get it while you can," or "strike while the iron is hot." This oversimplified advice on making money reinforces notions of scarcity, and could kill a good thing. When you have finally tapped into the prosperity consciousness, don't let greed cut the benefits short.

History supports this way of thinking. Many New York restaurants were hard hit after 9/11, particularly those in the downtown Manhattan area, but not everyone was adversely affected by these attacks. When restaurant owners compared their business results in 2001 to those of 2000, most owners reported a decline of 20 to 40 percent, and some were forced to close. One of the most prominent owners had four restaurants in the downtown Union Square area. His restaurants were never cheap, but they always enjoyed a reputation for high quality, innovative cooking, and good value. He also pioneered a local non-profit organization that delivered leftover food to the homeless.

This restaurant owner reported 2001 sales equal to or slightly better than those of 2000. While most restaurants were reeling after the attacks in a declining economy, this downtown restaurateur not only kept his ground, but slightly increased his business. Other restaurants with food just as good, in great locations, suffered a sharp drop in business. How did he avoid that fate?

His reputation and his energy sphere (see chapter 10) were outstanding before 9/11. When the perception of the economy was better in New York City just before 9/11, he didn't take advantage of his customers, although he probably could have been charging more money for some items. When 9/11 occurred and the economy changed, his restaurants became a natural draw for people seeking comfort.

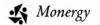

I have tried to emulate this model in managing my properties. I've attempted to treat tenants fairly, to make repairs as soon as possible, and to not quibble with tenants over anything, rent included. As mentioned previously, I have never been forced to go to court to collect rent from any tenant, despite having problems with a few. I've even received "thank you" notes from tenants after they've moved out. I've always obtained good rent for my buildings, but I've learned not to push the limits. If I have a tenant who is relatively trouble free, I almost never raise their rent, which could explain why my tenants seldom move.

In order to sustain your financial gains, you should probably tune out most, if not all, of the media's reporting on the economy — the "headline economy." The economy for each of us is a very individual thing, and it is sustained by our moment-to-moment efforts. Don't let anyone get you depressed, or hype you up about the economy, or use such opinions as a basis for what you can or cannot do. Use your gut feelings as a guide, not CNN or Fox News. Use the tools in this book to prosper and sustain your gains no matter what tragedy is playing out on the news.

Sustaining prosperity is ultimately about becoming a person who makes the required efforts over time to be *worthy* in every sense of the word — and this won't happen without seeing the connectivity of all energy and events in your life, and showing absolute respect to all.

Redefine Competition

It's time to take a new look at competition, and not just because we live in a global economy. The notion of not being competitive is tradition-ally thought to make you less effective, less productive, and unlikely to share in life's riches. But as you implement the principles of this book, your everyday life will be viewed less and less as a win-lose situation, especially as you decrease your focus on what other people have. The big surprise here is that you actually get a bigger piece of the pie this way. You begin to realize that the only person you really compete with is yourself. There is no need to compare what you have or where you are in life to anyone else. Why worry about where anyone else goes on vacation? Why envy anyone's pictures on Facebook or Instagram? Remove your life from any controlling matrix, feel great about where you are at this time, and project love onto everything and everyone in your path. You now have it made.

Where do you find yourself when you rise above traditional competitiveness? You see the process of recreating your financial situation with new perspective, and you enjoy this process, even if you struggle with it. You see yourself as just as safe and secure when things are happening as when they are finished, which is a huge blessing. The daily news, which may have impacted you heavily in the past, is put on the back burner of your life and hardly affects you at all. You are too busy creating the life of your dreams, and you are grateful for everything you create.

A prosperity consciousness will transform your present view on money — often a scarcity consciousness (based upon conditioning and life experience) — and propel you toward mastery of your financial fate. The benefits cannot be overstated: autonomy, new and exciting experiences, increased awareness, understanding how process works, and of course, increased wealth.

- Develop a prosperity consciousness and take control of your financial fate.
- Give respect and get respect — the "mirror effect."
- Find and develop your core strengths to expand your world.

- Ride the waves to prosperity by welcoming unpredictable circum-stances and embracing change.
- Take risks alone. Don't dilute creative energy by talking about it.
- Learn to sustain prosperity and compete only with yourself.
- View money as a by-product of your prosperity worthiness, not as a goal unto itself.

Chapter 6

Practice Generosity

Generosity is an interesting concept because like so many other things, it is not what many people think it to be. Being generous with others turns out to be not just a human privilege, but an incredibly useful tool to increase your wealth. This will become clear as you push the limits of your own generosity. While experimenting with generosity, you get the maximum energy effect when you give from the heart and are as sincere as possible. Don't be mechanical.

When I entered the workforce, I noticed that most people were incredibly cheap and were constantly complaining about not having enough money. I wondered why people behaved this way, and I was curious why these behaviors were often linked. The answer is fear — fear of being alone, fear of not paying the rent or mortgage, fear of not having enough to retire on, fear of not being able to afford to pay for your kids' college, fear of not keeping up with the neighbors, fear of getting older. Whatever it is, you can be sure that human beings attach a great deal of fear to it. I saw and experienced fear firsthand, and although I couldn't prove it then, I thought it was a limiting factor when it came to making and spending money wisely. I wanted to get rid of my fear attachments concerning money, but didn't know how to do it, so I became open with everyone, hoping that the answer would surface.

While sitting in a Miami Beach coffee shop having breakfast, I started a conversation with an elderly woman next to me. I inquired where she was from. She told me she was from southern California, but that she and her husband had moved to Florida three years prior because her husband was afraid of dying in an earthquake. I asked her where her husband was now, and she informed me sadly that he had died of a heart attack six months after moving to Florida. Fear is doubly damaging: The things we fear rarely occur, yet the energy of constant fear creates a negative energy field, and makes us vulnerable to other bad things happening. This woman's story triggered a huge epiphany for me about how fear operates, and helped me shed my own fears about money.

Many people are reluctant to be generous out of sheer habit — or from the absorption of miserly family conditioning (the "cheap gene"). I have always found it amusing and quite telling how people place such great importance on small monetary triumphs. In fact, the value placed on saving money or getting a bargain has become a national obsession. "Black Friday" commonly results in violent stampedes at some stores.

I spent a summer weekend with old friends at a Long Island beach house. One of the guests had made a lot of money in the stock market. He spent most of that beautiful weekend in the living room nervously watching stock market related shows; he barely spent any time on the beach at all. While that was significant on its own, he told me something even more revealing. He complained that it sometimes took him one-to-two hours to find a parking spot in his Upper East Side Manhattan neighborhood. I asked him why he didn't just put his car in a garage. His response: "Oh, I just couldn't give them that kind of money." I know garages in Manhattan are expensive and overpriced, but this guest spent a large part of the weekend trying to impress everyone with how rich he was!

I had a wealthy friend named Ann whom I met at one of my favorite parts of Central Park — the pond by 72nd street right off Fifth Avenue. I frequently went to this beautiful part of Central Park to contemplate nature and my future. Ann was elderly then, but we had a rapport that transcended our huge age difference. When I think about it now, I realize how much I liked her energy. My girlfriend at the time used to poke fun at me for spending time with her because of her age. She thought I was wasting my time, but I didn't see it that way. Ann's chronological age was irrelevant to me because she was fascinating, unique, and so much fun to be with. She was born in France but had come to the United States to marry an American around the time of World War II. She was the product of a bygone era, and I loved to hear stories about things that were legendary to me, like what pre-war France was all about. She had been a fashion designer for Vogue, and had been at parties with people like Greta Garbo and Marlene Dietrich. She had always traveled the world, even in her sixties and seventies. She had just divorced her husband at quite an advanced age, a move I found quite gutsy. She had what the French like to call *joie de vivre,* but she also had some very strange ideas about money. Ann lived in a beautiful and gracious pre-war coop just off Central Park. I was pretty certain she had no money problems of her own, but she could be downright cheap with other people.

Ann became hurt and went to the hospital. She called me at my office and asked for help getting home, so I immediately left work to get her. She was touched by this and said, "I'm going to get you a great present for Christmas." Getting rewarded was not my motivation for helping her, nor did I care about receiving anything from her for Christmas, but the holiday was just a few weeks away and she presented me with a beautifully wrapped present. I was quite surprised when I opened the box. Ann had given me a calendar for the next year — a Citibank calendar she had obviously gotten for free.

One of my former officemates also had some confusing and strange ideas about spending money that were revealed when we were walking to lunch at a nearby steakhouse. My colleague, a successful mortgage broker, was talking about her investment banker husband. She tried hard to impress me that she and her husband could afford anything.

We arrived at the steakhouse and I ordered a steak. She ordered a hamburger platter, which wouldn't have been unusual had she not just mentioned that she was in the mood for steak. When the waiter left, I asked her why she hadn't ordered the steak. "Oh, I don't want to spend the money for that." I was taken aback but didn't say a word; people show themselves to us in small ways. I made a mental note that this woman had some serious money issues. She was doing more than saving for a rainy day. *She was saving for the apocalypse.* Not only was her action at the steakhouse disagreeable, it was totally unnecessary. Her comments about money were an early warning sign that she was disturbed emotionally. I was right about that, too, and I later found out how disturbed she was.

It is rare to find anyone who has a healthy, balanced attitude toward money. Many people are in perpetual awe of money regardless of how much they have. They tend to have no clue as to money's true function due to its mythical allure embedded in most people's consciousness.

It doesn't have to be this way. You can be freer with your money, show generosity in all your dealings, and benefit financially.

I used the principle of generosity to acquire a new car. I live in Manhattan, and am aware that owning a car is not a necessity — but I enjoy driving and have always loved cars. I also believe we should try to experience the things we love. I had never owned a convertible, but I could see myself driving one fast with the top down playing my favorite music.

I calculated the cost of a car lease, insurance, and a garage to be about one thousand dollars a month. Since I wanted to enjoy this vehicle without worrying about the monthly cost for at least a year, I needed a starting lump sum of fifteen- to twenty-thousand dollars. I put the principles of energy to work. I was convinced that the energy of having exactly what I desired would provide me with a way to continue owner-ship beyond the first year. I found the car I wanted — a Jeep Wrangler Sport with a large engine and a killer surround-sound stereo. The car fit me like a glove in every way. All I needed was the money.

Around the same time, a stockbroker phoned me to discuss a partic-ular communication stock he liked, and suggested that I invest several thousand dollars in it. I didn't know much about that stock and was not actively involved in the stock market, so I thought about his suggestion for several days. I realized there was no way that buying several thou-sand dollars of the stock would earn me the sum I needed, so I decided to take a much larger risk; I bought stock options with the same few thousand dollars.

And that wasn't all. I decided to conduct a little experiment: While I continually visualized myself driving that car, I decided that I needed

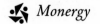

to be incredibly generous with everyone who crossed my path. I was asking the universe for a substantial benefit: the funds for the exact car I wanted; I needed to demonstrate my generosity first. This was crucial to access the energy needed to obtain that car.

Shortly after buying those options, I heard from close relatives who wanted to spend a weekend in Manhattan. I offered to pay for their favorite Manhattan hotel with a room facing Central Park, which was their preference. The stock I owned jumped two points the day after I spoke to them. My relatives came the next weekend and I treated them to dinner every night they were here. I made sure to tip the waiters generously, and also gave money to every street person or panhandler who asked. At the weekend's conclusion, I hired a stretch limousine to take them to the airport. I will never forget how happy they looked when I met them at their hotel with the limo, and rode with them for several blocks before getting out. Their enthusiasm was only enhanced because they had never been in that kind of car before. They left town and I never heard the end of it. They repeatedly told me and their friends that their New York weekend had been one of the highlights of their life.

I watched that stock very carefully in the next few weeks. It was a rocky ride, but I felt connected to the energy of that stock. I viewed it as a means to obtain a very specific goal, which was the exact car I wanted with no compromise. I continued to give money to every street person who actively approached me, and I welcomed the opportunity to take friends out to dinner. Before I could look around, the stock had doubled in price, which meant I made about seventeen thousand dollars on an initial twenty-five-hundred dollar investment. I sold the stock and leased the car. I still have that car today, and it gives me enormous pleasure every time I drive it. Knowing how I obtained it only compounds the pleasure. That car came straight from the purest energy I could access. Most people think the car looks brand new, although it's actually more than eight years old. I attribute those comments to the energy I accessed to obtain that car. Since it came from *the source* (see chapter 12), the car retains an uncanny, fresh quality.

Having a car in Manhattan could be construed as a luxury to some, but I never take that car for granted. I have a big smile on my face whenever I see my car's round headlights staring at me, and that's in no small measure due to the way I obtained it. I love to drive around New York with the top up or down. I play my music as loud as I want. I take frequent jaunts into the beautiful countryside an hour north of New York to hike on the Appalachian Trail. I think of that car as having great energy. I can't imagine anything but good times connected to it, so I feel totally protected while I am in it. If you asked me to trade that Jeep for a Ferrari at no cost to me, the answer would be a resounding *No.* My theory that the energy of having exactly what I wanted would allow me to keep the car beyond the first year without worrying about paying for it has proven absolutely true.

I also used the principle of generosity in a recent real estate project, a loft conversion that stretched me financially and creatively. I put a great deal of financial resources at risk because I had faith in the outcome, and I thought the potential was enormous. While in this risk mode, I grabbed every opportunity to stretch my generosity with others. From an energy standpoint, it was clear what I was doing. I was putting my sincere and honest energy into a project in which I had a true strength and interest. In so doing, I was riding those waves and placing large resources at risk with a specific goal constantly in mind. It was anything but a sure thing, but it was a calculated risk — a perfect example of many of the principles in this book at work.

If this project were to culminate the way I envisioned, the financial balance of power would make a huge shift in my favor. The last three or four months of that project were crucial, so I monitored my energy very closely. I was conscious that although I was asking a great deal from the universe, I was not entitled to a positive result just because I was seeking one.

My actions became more and more directed every day. I started giving more. I will always remember going to an ATM on a very cold December Sunday. I parked my car in front of the bank and went in, and when I came out, a homeless person asked me for money. I looked at him, reached into my pocket, and without thinking about it, gave him twenty dollars. I don't think he realized it was more than a dollar for a few seconds after he took the bill. By that time, I was just getting into my jeep and starting the engine. When this man realized I had given him twenty dollars, he came running up to my car and started yelling, "God bless you! *God bless you!*" He chased my car halfway down the street yelling, "God Bless you" the whole way. I remember how moved I was by his reaction, so much so that I glowed for several days afterward.

I didn't feel that way because it flattered my ego to give a stranger twenty dollars, nor am I suggesting that I am a great person for doing this. Something else was going on. It hit me that my interaction with that homeless man could have profoundly affected and possibly even changed his perspective on life. I don't know what had led him to that point, or how long it had been since anyone had shown him that much generosity or kindness, or acknowledged his existence as a human being on this planet. It could have rekindled all kinds of hopes previously buried by a string of bad experiences. Another thing dawned on me, too: I had a lot in common with that homeless person, even though I was not homeless. Just as that homeless person's life was placed at risk by his living on the streets, my life was at risk, but for other reasons. I was riding those waves with a lot at stake at that moment. The fates of both of us were up in the air; anything could have happened to either of us.

I realized that if I had the power to fundamentally change that person's life at that moment, he also possessed the power to change my life in a fundamental way by blessing me the way he had. Just as the smallest gesture or remark can make someone your lifetime enemy––the gift that keeps on giving––couldn't the converse be true? The energy of someone constantly blessing you could influence your life in a positive way without time limits. All of us possess that power regardless of class or economic status.

In chapter 1, I shared the story about Ned's lawyer who thought he was so powerful, but was reduced to mumbling incoherently in that will contest. We've all encountered people who think that their position, money, or connections give them the power to control a situation. Ned's lawyer did not possess the power he presumed he had, and the harsh reality is that nobody does. That power to affect the outcome can come through the most unlikely sources at the most unexpected times. In the case of that will contest, the power came through me, a young and inexperienced lawyer. I was someone who, to the other lawyers, was probably the most unexpected source of power — but it was not *my* power in any real sense. That power does not belong to anyone, and if you should try to capture it, like many good things in life, it will vanish as mysteriously as it came. The most we can expect is to have access to that power, and our access is limited by many factors, not the least of which is respect.

When I thought about my energy exchange with that homeless man, other elements intrigued me, too. I couldn't remember for the life of me when anyone had blessed me, and certainly not with that much pure love and enthusiasm. Of course, people give to all kinds of charities, and they often give a lot more than twenty dollars. However, it is rare to see and feel the impact of what is given so directly. The impact on me was strong. Also, there was no bureaucracy to dilute the experience, so in a very real sense, we were both gift giver and recipient.

The next weekend was bitterly cold. I found myself running to a bank cash machine again with my jeep double-parked. An elderly woman with a cup in hand opened the door for me when I left; I don't remember seeing her when I entered. She asked me for money, too, and as I looked at her face, I was reminded of my mother — or anybody's mother. My next thought was of how much I would *not* like my mother to be begging outside of a bank on such a bitterly cold day. I reached into my pocket and gave her twenty dollars, just as I had done the week before, but she saw the amount immediately. As I dashed to my double-parked car, she ran after me shouting, "God bless you! *God bless you! God bless you!*" I was thus blessed by two total strangers within the course of one week. These people were homeless, and regarded by many as worthless, disposable, and powerless. They were not considered to be the kind of people who could influence anything, let alone the course of events for you or me. How did I feel during that time when my fate was also being determined? What kind of power or energy did these homeless people impart to me? *I felt blessed.*

Several weeks later, I was invited to a friend's birthday party at an Italian restaurant. The birthday girl was a friend of the restaurant owner, so you can imagine the food we had. All kinds of special appetizers, any entree we wanted, fantastic desserts, and free-flowing French champagne were available. About fifteen people came to enjoy various parts of a full-course meal, and the check was divided up among everyone except the birthday girl. I had a great time at the party, so when the bill was presented, I grabbed it, having decided to pay for everyone. (I wasn't kidding when I spoke about taking risks and experimenting with what happens!)

I was shocked when I looked at the bill because the owner, who had joined us for the party, had generously reduced an estimated fifteen-hundred-dollar tab to just three-hundred-dollars. When I announced to the table that I would be paying, nobody, including me, knew about this reduction. The reaction of most guests to my gesture was disbelief. I was not surprised by their response, because I knew that by offering to pay, I was threatening their belief systems. Whether the guests were rich or poor — and there was a smattering of each with most in the middle — people had been taught to reach into their pockets only as a last resort. Hardly anyone is conditioned to view the chance to spend money on other people as an opportunity.

But I was conducting an experiment. I consciously made this generous effort to see whether any repercussions would occur in my ongoing loft conversion project. The theory I was testing: Can you create an energy field to directly influence your life's events? If you can, it is surely one of the best uses of free will there is.

This is the opposite of playing the lottery, where you and ten million people vie for the same prize with an attitude that bespeaks powerlessness. What you say and do every moment contributes to an energy buildup that directly impacts everything you are involved with. The real estate project that was nearing completion should have been affected by my generosity at the restaurant. I was asking a great deal from the universe with this project, which, if successful, would catapult me financially, like winning the lottery.

I now know — not think — that if my behavior during this crucial time period had been anything less than generous to the extreme, the events I wanted would never have occurred.

A postscript on that party: Another year went by, and that same birthday girl had a party at the same Italian restaurant, with mostly the same guests as the year before. When the bill came that year, I waited to see what would happen. I didn't offer to pay for everyone. Two curious things happened that revealed a lot about human nature: The bill somehow ended up in my hands, and I was expected to collect all the money. And not one person remembered my gesture of the year before; nobody suggested I be excused from paying.

I was a little drunk on champagne at that year's party, so the tip I calculated probably wasn't sufficient. I called the birthday girl the next day to discuss this. Even though the tip was just shy of 20 percent, we were a demanding lot, and I thought the servers deserved a larger gratuity. The birthday girl got angry at me for not leaving enough money, even though none of the other guests seemed to care how much money they threw down, and were completely indifferent to how much of a tip was left. I did care, so two days later, I went back to the restaurant, spoke to the manager, and offered to leave an extra tip. The manager was incredulous that I was making this effort, but I insisted. I wrote a thank you note to our waiter, and slipped it into an envelope with sixty dollars. When I handed the envelope back to the manager, he took it, looked me straight in the eyes, and said, *"God bless you."* Those words only confirmed that I was doing the right thing, even if no one else at that party knew, cared, or understood the energy principles at work.

Constantly update, rearrange, and refine your ideas about generosity, just like with other areas of your life. Attempt to make those who cross your path feel more than well taken care of, because that's how you like to feel, too. And in this world where we are all challenged by so many things, where elements of civilized behavior are routinely ignored, people are very appreciative when they are treated well. As you become more concerned with not just meeting, but with surpassing other people's needs, you'll notice that your needs are not just met, but considerably exceeded. This is directly related to your consistent daily efforts at generosity. Unlike the way it is for most people, regard the chance to be generous as an opportunity. This behavior creates good feelings and energy for all because money is love and joy when spread around. Generosity attracts financial opportunities that elude or remain unavailable to others, and even more important, *it makes your life so pleasant.* Experiment with giving in a way that is comfortable to you, and observe the results.

When you are routinely generous, you start to internalize the fact that there is abundance all around you, and it's no big deal. Once you overcome your conditioned fear of not having enough, being destitute, or facing the apocalypse, you can give what you want when you want and feel fine doing it. You can also voluntarily, and with pleasure, let go of money when it's demanded, rather than hang on to it as long as possible. It's an incredibly freeing feeling. More than anything, it confirms your faith in the universe and your control over your own fate. Life doesn't get much better than that, and I am convinced that the gods bestow special favors on someone who can let go of money when faced with a life-affirming opportunity. This belief system of generosity is extremely powerful and gives you an immediate energy advantage. It's a no-brainer: Be generous with everyone!

That real estate project succeeded and gave me the huge financial boost I had envisioned — in no small part due to the generosity I showed along the way. There was something else I realized once the dust had cleared. It was terrific that I could experience a new level of control over my finances, but with that new level of control came a new level of responsibility. If I wanted to maintain and expand control over my financial life, generosity toward everyone would have to be not just sustained, but enhanced. That sense of generosity expanded to include giving my time to others, which is perhaps more precious than any monetary offering.

If you want to become generous, here's a simple suggestion for every-day behavior: look at your server's face the next time you go into a restaurant. If they've had a particularly bad day, you'll feel it. Assuming the service is adequate, offer an especially big tip, and then watch the server for a reaction. Make a real connection with that person. Feel their energy and gratitude directed toward you. You'll have just made a major difference in that person's day. There's a huge ricochet effect, too. You may influence the way that server treats every person they encounter that same day — and maybe tomorrow and the next day, too. In the process, you allow yourself to be blessed by that person with-out any time limit. Positive energy accrues more quickly than you'd think. When you start feeling comfortable making efforts like this all the time, and when other energy factors are aligned, you'll have consciously set in motion a drastic change to your finances. *Watch out. It's going to be a wild ride!*

Your reality (health, wealth, relationships) is ultimately determined by your belief system, which operates in your life like the hard drive on your computer. This is great news because you can use generosity to enhance your wealth, and every other part of your life, too. This process, which incorporates patience, sincerity, sustained effort, and love, is not just eye-opening; it will transform you to another level of consciousness.

- Think of generosity as a tool you can use to increase your wealth.
- Eliminate your fear of being generous.
- Experiment with generosity and observe the change to your finances, and your well-being.
- Expand your notion of generosity to include not just money, but time.

Chapter 7

Watch for Signs / Cycle Out

Watching for signs and cycling out are critical concepts because they help you monitor the energy around you. By watching for signs, I don't mean the billboards on the way to work; I mean noticing everyone and everything that comes into your life, every minute of every day, and then taking appropriate action. You can't be asleep at the wheel.

Since your fate is determined on a moment-to-moment basis, being tuned in to your environment allows you to shape your financial world; otherwise your fate becomes random. Cycling out is related to watching for signs, but it refers to the right time to move out of a financial situation before it turns bad.

I saw how important these principles could be when my old landlord tried to convert my rental building into condominiums. In New York City's crazed real estate market, a conversion can create an opportunity for tenants to buy one's apartment at a substantial discount, but my well-known landlord took a hard-line position. He refused to negotiate with the tenants at all, and tried to convert the building by selling the vacant apartments to outsiders at full market value. If he was able to sell just 15 percent of the total units to outsiders, that could change the building's status from rental to condominium — and more than 15 percent of the apartments were vacant. Most landlords would not consider a conversion to be financially successful with only 15 percent of the apartments purchased, but my landlord, an old time New York real estate company, behaved differently because it was rich, well entrenched, and greedy.

Once we were notified of the planned conversion to condominiums, we formed a tenants' committee and began the search for an attorney. This 1960s era building was twenty-one floors high with about two-hundred-and-fifty apartments. I had always liked that building because, besides being close to the United Nations, its architecture reflected the optimistic attitude of the era, and almost all the rooms were large — no incredibly shrinking bedrooms there. I volunteered to serve on the seven-member steering committee, since I had a strong affinity for the building and wanted to protect it from the landlord's manipulation.

A short time before the attempted conversion, I obtained my apartment in an unusual fashion by using the landlord's negative energy. It was a fantastic space with great light, dramatic views, and a big wrap-around terrace and garden. I was thrilled to be living there, and I still live there today.

The steering committee was responsible for interviewing and selecting the attorney to represent the tenants and negotiate with the landlord. The committee members preferred, and hired, a very mild mannered attorney, but I disagreed with their choice from the start. I had had some previous business dealings with the landlord, and he made Darth Vader seem like a nice guy. The attorney I wanted was a well-known litigator who had prevailed in some of the toughest legal battles in New York City against big landlords. He was an extremely bright guy with a sense of humor, and a slightly rough demeanor who I thought was perfect for dealing with our shark-like landlord. He was interviewed by the steering committee, but they rejected him despite his qualifications, for reasons I think were related to his aggressive character. Interestingly enough, that aggressiveness earned him a huge victory against Donald Trump in a building on Central Park South, as well as a more recent twenty-five-million dollar buy-out for a few hold-out tenants obstructing a huge West Side Manhattan development site.

Our generic and less threatening attorney began negotiations with the landlord. After several unsuccessful meetings, it was apparent he wasn't getting anywhere. Our landlord repeatedly threatened that he was going to convert the building around us by selling vacant apartments to outsiders. If the landlord succeeded in that plan, he stood to reap a huge financial gain without the tenants benefiting at all. That was just plain unfair.

Our attorney continued the dead-end negotiations over the next six months. We would skirmish with the landlord, attempt to set up meetings through our attorney, and then the meetings would be either canceled or unproductive. Our attorney's attitude became defeatist. He actually told us at a tenants' meeting that it wouldn't be such a bad thing if the landlord converted the building around us.

I was up in arms, but interestingly, it didn't seem to upset any of the other tenants. I've noticed that people tend to automatically put too much faith in the opinions of professionals — a big mistake if they are ill-informed, or have bad motives.

The passivity of this tenant group and its failure to pick up any signs that something was wrong was appalling to me. It reminded me of how people didn't react to the Nazis' signals of their intentions before World War II. I lived in a multi-family high-rise building in Manhattan, yet I was the only person who picked up any signs of something amiss.

I continued to raise serious concerns about our attorney's advice. I suggested we change attorneys to my original choice, and I became the target of other tenants' attacks. One of these tenants even suggested that I was motivated by a potential kickback. It never ceases to amaze me how off the mark people can be, especially when their beliefs are threatened. This state of inertia continued for another few months, and the other tenants continued to attack my motivation for changing attorneys, but I didn't care. I relentlessly insisted that we change attorneys before the situation worsened.

My efforts made a slight impact when the president of the steering committee approached me in confidence, and admitted that he had misgivings about our attorney's performance. It took him about a year to see this — and he was a successful businessman who ran his own company. He suggested we meet with the attorney I initially preferred, and I gladly set up the appointment.

At the meeting, the attorney I had preferred reviewed the developments in our conversion process. His comments were clear, insightful, intelligent, and hard for the president to refute in any way. Just as I had been insisting for a year, the new attorney thought our current attorney's behavior was strange. It turned out that there had been many ways for us to defeat the landlord's conversion, and he outlined about ten steps that should have been taken all along. Contrary to what our current attorney had claimed, the new attorney spelled out the great harm that would fall to tenants if the building was converted around us. If the landlord was ignoring us, we had every incentive to actively defeat his plan.

The committee president admitted there was something wrong with our current attorney's advice. He called a special steering committee

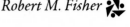

meeting to recommend changing attorneys. He was convinced we should change attorneys to the one I initially recommended.

The other steering committee members seemed shocked at this development. While they viewed me as a pariah because I refused to stop talking about this issue, they had absolute respect for the president, who ran his own company, was much older than me, spoke with an impressive British accent, and lived in one of the choicest penthouses in the building.

After the president spoke, someone seconded his request for a vote on whether to change attorneys from our old defeatist attorney to the new one. Then every one of those steering committee members voted to change attorneys! I could see that they were doing it grudgingly, but I didn't care. The looks on their faces showed how much they hated to admit I was right, and I would be lying if I said I didn't feel some sense of personal vindication.

We fired our former attorney and hired the new one. Our new attorney and his staff quickly got into the fray. Remember those vacant apartments that, if sold to outsiders, could amount to 15 percent of the units — the amount needed to convert the building to condominiums? Our new attorney launched a detailed investigation into the identity of those outside purchasers, which was something our old attorney had never done or even suggested. He found some curious irregularities. Most of those who had contracted to buy those vacant apartments were in some way related to the landlord — distant relatives, former employees, or people with some other association. Under New York law, purchasers of those vacant apartments had to be completely unrelated to the landlord; the vast majority of those sales to outsiders were invalidated. As a result, the conversion plan was declared invalid by the

New York State Attorney General's office. The rental character of the building was preserved, the landlord was defeated, and we prevented him from manipulating us financially.

Had I not been watching the signs around me, the landlord could have caused us tremendous financial harm. Not one of the other two-hundred-and-fifty tenants had thought anything was wrong, *or* taken action.

The benefits of keenly observing my surroundings were illustrated clearly when I had two real estate projects close on the same day. The finalization of those two projects contributed to a large change in my financial status. I deliberately scheduled these two events on the same day because I wanted to feel their total effect in a concentrated time-frame, like a financial energy blast.

I decided to go swimming the morning after these closings. I often look to the comments of strangers and everyday experiences to indicate whether I am where I should be at a given moment. On my way home, I bought breakfast at a bakery. Now picture this: I was in my sweats, my hair was wet from the pool, and I was leaving the bakery to go home. A homeless guy on the corner looked up at me and said, "You just pulled off a big one, didn't you?" I was floored and stopped in my tracks. I had never seen this person before, yet he picked up that energy from me, and he was right on the money. I had indeed "pulled off a big one" just the day before.

At the time I started writing this book, I needed to buy some jeans, so I went to Soho, a downtown Manhattan area filled with shops and art galleries. I went to a store I liked, not just for the unusual Italian merchandise, but because the store owner had good energy. I had spoken with him on several occasions, and discovered that he had overcome a disadvantaged background to own this men's store that featured unusual and interesting European clothes. He was attitude free and had no resentment about his past. I always admire people who have overcome obstacles life has thrown their way without complaining, or labeling themselves a victim.

There I was, looking for a pair of jeans — when I was writing this book about energy. I saw several pairs of jeans I liked, and I tried them on. The first pair was too tight, but the second pair fit me like a glove. I looked at the label. The name was L'energie. It was a new Italian brand then, and as you might guess, I bought the jeans. What were the odds of my selecting a pair of jeans with the name "Energy" just when I started to write a book about energy? Was it just some kind of coincidence, or was it confirmation that I was doing just what I was meant to at that moment?

I became interested in the stock market again after it tumbled so dramatically in late 2008. I was watching one bank stock in particular that had been mercilessly trashed. This stock went from eighteen dollars to about $3.50 in less than six months. When the stock was at that low point, I decided the time might be right for a purchase, but I was away on a trip. I tried to make an electronic transfer from my bank to the brokerage company so I could purchase the stock while I was out of town. No one seemed able to make the electronic transfer happen. I felt that some force was preventing me from buying the stock, so I deferred to it. *Maybe this is a sign I shouldn't buy it.* I decided to go for a swim and forget about it until I returned to New York. I got back about ten days later, made the transfer to my brokerage account, and was able to buy that same stock, but the price had dropped even further; it was now trading at only $1.50. Within two weeks that stock went back up to three dollars, and I promptly sold it, making a 100 percent profit.

"Being in the right place at the right time" is often cited as the reason that some people, and not others, are able to take advantage of financial opportunities. This notion suggests that it is all random — a kind of luck that some people have and others do not. Luck is not random. It is actually created by watching the signs around you.

When you pay attention to the signs around you, you receive constant feedback from your environment about the propriety of your every action. With practice, you can be in the right place at the right time almost all the time.

Cycle Out

The concept of cycling out is related to watching the signs around you. If you become more attuned to the signs in your everyday life, your experiences will acquire new flavor and clarity. All experiences have a beginning, a middle, and an end. Knowing that cycles are perfectly natural could not be more important, as economic cycles shift rapidly, like everything else today. Cycling out refers to choosing the right time to leave a financial situation or project, because you sense that things are changing in a fundamental way. You get that first whiff, you watch the situation closely, and you get a strong sense that things are starting to turn or end — so you cycle out.

Life is about constant change, but change can cause anxiety or fear, especially if you are thrown out of a comfortable situation. If you view change as a healthy thing, you learn to not just live with it, but to ride the wave of change to your advantage. Problems arise when you put a bubble around the things or people you want to keep the same forever.

By cycling out of a situation after you have substantially reached your goals and when you begin to detect the situation changing, you show respect and faith — respect for the principles discussed in this book, and faith that you are creating new opportunities as you cycle out of old ones. When you cycle out, you separate yourself from the majority of people who hang on until the bitter end, and often get clobbered in the process. Anyone who has stayed in the stock market during a dramatic downturn, or experienced a rapid decrease in real estate values, can attest to that.

I always try to cycle out of projects near the top of the market, but I don't need to get every last penny of gain. I set my goals at a certain level, but I also like to leave something for the next person. I feel very good about this approach, because it confirms my faith that there are more opportunities to come.

When I decided to cycle out of a downtown Manhattan loft I had purchased, the property had increased in value by 80 percent in the two years I had owned it. Although the value of that loft was still rising, it had increased so rapidly that I thought future appreciation would not be as great. I decided to cycle out. At the same time, I focused on a new and much larger project in a less developed area where I thought the appreciation would be better. By selling that loft when I did, I was able to buy that much larger property in an area that had yet to see dramatic growth.

I was gratified to learn that the person who bought my loft has seen an increase in value of almost 75 percent since I sold it to him. In that same period, the much larger project I bought saw an increase of 120 percent, after I renovated it with considerable care and effort. And because the new property was so much larger, my net rental income increased tenfold compared to what it had been from that individual loft.

Keenly observe your surroundings on a moment-to-moment basis so you can create and preserve your wealth. This is an effort that will never terminate, but watching the signs is something you become comfortable with and learn to eventually like. It keeps you rooted in the present, which is an invaluable gift. You can then cycle out of opportunities naturally when they have run their course, and have no regret.

- Watch for signs in your life to guide you and build wealth.
- Be attuned to your environment and create your own luck.
- Don't hang on too long while waiting for the last drop of opportunity. Cycle out when you've met your goals, and leave some benefit for the next person.

CHAPTER 8

CONVERT NEGATIVE ENERGY TO MONEY

Converting negative energy to money is a bonanza seldom contemplated, but it is like striking oil in your own backyard. You take a commodity that is in abundant supply — others' negative energy — dissect it from an energy standpoint, and then reshape it into a financial or power bonus for yourself.

Since much of the resistance you encounter in the business world comes in the form of negative energy, knowing how to handle negative energy is crucial. Remember Ned's lawyer in Chapter 1 who couldn't fathom losing the will contest to me when I was so young and inexperienced? Although I wasn't fully aware of it then, I used his negative energy to create a windfall for myself and for my client.

Negative energy comes in many forms: People who are manipulative or malicious emit a certain kind of negative energy; passive-aggressive types produce abundant negative energy, too. Negative energy often masquerades as power, status, or controlling behavior, but it invariably hides fear, frustration, and/or insecurity. By exercising their so-called power over you, other people emit negative energy, develop a sense of entitlement, and set themselves up for a fall — and the bigger the sense of entitlement, the bigger the fall. As you become more familiar with this process, you'll be better able to recognize this. That's the first step.

You have no control over others' behavior, nor should you aspire to. However, you can develop much more control over your reaction to anyone's behavior as you become more detached and assume the role of the observer. Rather than succumb to or back away from others' negative energy, you have a new choice: you can convert others' negative energy to your own financial well-being. It is a subtle process, to turn around and harness others' negative energy for your own financial gain. It occurs in your mind and your consciousness first, then it manifests in your physical reality. It also involves a whole new definition of what it means to be powerful, because anyone can convert other people's negative energy to money and become powerful.

The process of converting other people's negative energy to financial gain is based on *energy advantage.* You automatically acquire the energy advantage in every situation where negative energy is thrust at or around you, provided your own energy is relatively blame free. If you react in a vengeful way, or provoke the negative energy through your own culpable acts, none of this will work. The energy advantage is automatic for two very important reasons:

1. A continuing conflict between dark and light, positive and negative, exists in the universe and within each of us. The universe ultimately chooses light over darkness so that life is affirmed. Thus, if someone thrusts negative energy at or around you and you refuse to yield to it, the universe rewards you with an energy advantage at that moment. This advantage must be used soon after the event or it will disappear.

2. The energy advantage accrues to you because negative energy boomerangs back to the perpetrator, creating an energy vacuum

(see chapter 9: Instant Karma). The place where you convert negative energy to your financial gain is in that energy void. Using this awareness, here is how the process works:

Step 1: Sense the negative energy directed at or around you.

Step 2: Zero in on the event containing that malevolent energy, and sense the full power of that energy.

Step 3: Take that power for your own, since it is directed at or around you (the energy advantage).

Step 4: Consciously ask yourself what financial opportunities you want to create or enhance.

Step 5: Consciously direct that energy toward that financial goal.

Step 6: Let go and allow what you want to manifest.

Approach the time factor with humility and patience when you start working with this, because being in a hurry for goals to manifest will work against the process. The time it takes for conversion is generally reduced as your familiarity with this process increases, and you'll get better at targeting where the energy goes, too. The good news is that the more malevolent the energy is, the bigger the boost you get toward your goal.

Whenever anyone says or does something to me that is negative, this instantly flashes in my mind: *I've got the energy advantage here so what do I want to do with it?* I can now do what was seemingly impossible before. Instead of getting angry at people who direct negative energy my way, I bless them, because they have just conferred a huge benefit upon me.

At an early age, I became aware of the effects of negative energy. My father worked with my grandfather and cousin in a thriving local beverage business that I visited frequently. Even at the tender age of four, I sensed that the cousin had it in for my dad and was treating him in a malevolent way. The cousin was sarcastic, and he and his wife, who often spent time there, seemed to get enormous pleasure from belittling my father and ordering him around. My father was young at the time, and he was reluctant to associate anything negative with his idealistic notion of family. My grandfather was too busy running the business to notice, was purposely oblivious, or possibly enjoyed the conflict.

Nonetheless, my cousin's negative energy propelled my dad out of that store faster than he had originally planned. He doubled up on his studies and landed a much better job in a new field. My grandfather's business went downhill shortly thereafter. A large chain store opened across the street, slashed prices on the same goods, and my grandfather and cousin were out of business within a year. My grandfather went on to a totally new business and prospered, and my father did well in his new field. My cousin took the loss very hard and suffered a nervous breakdown. He never fully recovered.

I have frequently used this energy conversion process to produce favorable results. When I was making the transition from law to the real estate business, I converted my officemate's negative energy into a lucrative new real estate opportunity. I shared an office suite at that time with other real estate professionals, including commercial real estate and mortgage brokers. I was on friendly terms with the five other members of the office suite, and would occasionally draft the leases for their real estate deals. I did most of this work for a commercial broker named George. He was proud of his success, and valued money quite highly. I didn't share those views but it didn't matter, because we got along well for about two years. I had seen his attitude about money result in frequent attempts at manipulation, downright nastiness, and fights with other members of the office. When he came into my office to let off steam after those fights, I usually just listened, shook my head, and laughed. I didn't take sides, but noted his character traits for the record.

We were once working on a commercial lease that was taking a long time to finalize, and George was becoming very nervous. He occupied an office three doors down from mine, and every morning he would burst into my office while I was having breakfast to cajole me about that deal. I became annoyed at the anxiety he tried to project on me. I told him I was 99 percent sure the deal we were working on would be completed, but that didn't comfort him. It was unfathomable why he was so nervous, as he was downright rich in his own right, and was married to the president of a local university. Their combined salaries were enormous.

He turned cold as ice to me after this discussion, which was the opposite of his past behavior. I wasn't surprised because I had seen this behavior in him before, though never directed at me. He also made it clear that he wasn't going to refer any more legal business my way. He did not know that I couldn't have cared less about getting more legal work from him, since I was not the slightest bit dependent upon him financially. In fact, my hope was that in a short time, I would be 100 percent out of practicing law. As it turned out, his negative behavior toward me unwittingly facilitated that goal. He had no idea about the extent of my real estate endeavors because I never gratuitously talked about those projects, and he had no need to know.

His negative behavior intensified, and it became unpleasant to go to work. The secretary we shared couldn't understand his change of attitude. I know she liked me a lot, felt badly about his treatment of me, and thought his sudden coldness was unjustified. Three weeks went by and the deal he had been so nervous about finally closed. This was no surprise to me, but his cold attitude toward me never abated. If anything, his ego was bruised because I had been right. His malevolence intensified. My only consolation was that I knew I would be leaving that office soon.

I came into the office late one day to find our secretary on the phone with a hospital where George had been taken after having difficulty breathing. He had almost died, and the doctors thought something was wrong with his lungs. It turned out to be a short hospital stay, and I don't know what the long-term outcome was, since I soon moved out of that office and had no reason to keep in touch.

A different but very interesting fate awaited me. I had just started to look for a new real estate project, had a very specific idea in mind, and had decided to convert my officemate's negative energy to advance my goal. I was conscious of all the coldness, malice, and negative energy he had directed at me daily. I was particularly aware that he wanted to hurt me financially, since this was his way of wielding power over others. I also knew he didn't have the power to harm me, because I had done nothing wrong except speak the truth as I saw it. I started to look for my next new project with this awareness.

I was willing to be patient as I was looking for a rare type of factory building to convert into loft apartments in an area that was no longer "under the radar." Things happened much faster than I could have ever imagined, and I found a building that was just about perfect after only two or three days of looking. My construction manager had a look of amazement in his eyes when I showed him that building. It was almost the exact type of loft project that we had spoken about, and it was located in a great developing neighborhood in Brooklyn. We had already completed three projects in the same vicinity.

We had both thought it would take anywhere from six months to a year to find this new deal, if we could find it at all. However, our calculations were based on a neutral playing field. Unknown to my officemate George, his extreme, relentless, malevolent energy toward me created a void. I was able to enter that energy void, convert his negative energy, and tilt the odds strongly in my favor.

I was very fortunate to obtain that building, but that was only the first of many steps needed to renovate, finance, and market the project. Like anything that has taken me to the next level, that project proved to be more time consuming, more costly, and more precarious than I had initially thought. It involved a substantial amount of personal risk. I had to go into the great unknown and ride the waves. However, when it was all over and the dust had settled, this project took me to a new financial plateau, and *I was 100 percent out of the legal field.*

Remember the apartment I had been living in when the landlord tried to convert the building into condominiums? I obtained that apartment using the landlord's negative energy. I first lived in a studio in the same building after I graduated from law school. It was a nice-sized alcove studio, but I knew there were some amazing apartments on the upper floors of my building with wraparound terraces. As a young attorney just out of law school, I had a fantasy about Manhattan living, and those penthouse-like apartments fit right in.

I hadn't lived in my studio long before I discovered that almost every tenant had extremely negative things to say about our landlord. I was aware of the animosity between landlords and tenants in New York City, but this seemed unusually bad. I soon understood what the tenants meant. Although ours was considered to be a luxury building (which in New York usually means overpriced), the service was haphazard and management seemed intentionally nasty.

I became acquainted with one of my neighbors while living in that studio, a woman in her late fifties. I initially met her because she complained that my stereo was too loud, and I'm sure it was! We reached a truce and then became friends. She lived elsewhere and used her two-bedroom apartment as an office for her interior design business.

The landlord had always known she wasn't living in that apartment, but didn't seem to care when she had leased it years ago in a weaker real estate market. And she was one of the few tenants in the building who considered the managing agent a friend.

My neighbor seemed despondent when I saw her a few months later. She said the landlord was trying to evict her, claiming she made improper use of her apartment by having her business there. "But didn't he know about and consent to your business use all along?" I asked her. Apparently so, but the landlord seemed intent on getting rid of her so he could get a higher paying tenant. Of course, she had been there a long time and had had no trouble paying the rent. I advised her to fight the eviction, since the landlord had previously consented to her non-residential use.

She hired an attorney but never fought it all the way. She finally agreed to leave the apartment after a year. This very rich landlord was trying to get rid of my neighbor out of pure greed, and one of the landlord's executives was a supposed friend who had accommodated my neighbor's growing business five years earlier, and moved her to this larger two-bedroom space. That same friend was now betraying her. I felt badly that someone as malevolent as our landlord could push my next-door neighbor around, a woman I had come to like very much. The landlord's negative energy offended me.

At the same time, I decided to get a larger apartment in my building. I wasn't sure exactly how to do it, since approaching the landlord directly would only place me on a dead end waiting list. Also, I wanted to take advantage of the landlord's huge reservoir of negative energy.

I asked the daytime doorman if he knew of anyone in a larger apartment who was moving out. I approached that particular doorman for help because I liked him, and because he had a certain energy I thought would be helpful. I told him I would love an apartment on one of the higher floors with a set back, open terrace. He looked at me and smirked, knowing how difficult it was to snag one of those incredible apartments, but he said he'd keep it in mind. I have always believed in going after exactly what I wanted, even if others called me a dreamer. If someone calls me that now I take it as a compliment, because they are really saying that I have vision.

I heard nothing about a new apartment for several months and became busy with other things. One day I got a call from the doorman who told me to talk to a guy on the 18th floor who was thinking of moving out.

I could hardly wait. I went up to the 18th floor the next night, walked into that apartment, and looked around with a weird sense of *déjà vu*. I stepped onto the forty-foot open terrace that wound around the apartment filled with planters and two huge trees. When I looked up at the top of my apartment building, I saw how the floors above had similar open terraces set back from one another, which made each of those apartments feel like a penthouse. Since I lived smack in the middle of Manhattan, the view was breathtaking and intense; it felt like a movie set with an undeniable sense of place, and that was New York City.

I was overwhelmed after walking out on that terrace, because I have always been a sucker for great views. I tried to remain calm, cool, and nonchalant about the whole thing, but I knew this was a very special apartment with incredibly positive and flowing energy. Every room, including the bedroom, opened onto that open, planted terrace. The interior was a bit neglected and painted with strange colors, but that could easily be fixed. I could see myself living there in a second.

We went back inside and talked about my host's situation. He turned out to be one of the most honorable and generous people I have ever met, and also one of the most intelligent. He was a Harvard educated attorney working for a lobbying group whose office was moving from Manhattan to Brooklyn. He didn't want to commute when he was in town because he traveled so extensively for work. He wanted to move to Brooklyn where he could walk to work. I didn't argue with him, even though his new Brooklyn office was only about a thirty-minute train ride from his current Manhattan apartment. I learned at a very early age that when the forces are working with you, do not question or stop them!

I steered the conversation to whether the two of us could force the landlord to transfer that apartment to me. He was more than willing to cooperate, since he was aware of the landlord's shabby treatment of tenants. We both expressed the desire to redress these wrongs if we could, and to use the landlord's negative energy to accomplish something good, such as transferring the apartment lease to me. I felt we were kindred spirits, even though we had never met before that night.

We discussed the best strategy for accomplishing the lease transfer. We rejected asking the landlord, because he would never voluntarily give me an apartment so desirable; the landlord put his own cronies in the best apartments. We were both aware of some recent court cases that allowed an existing tenant to compel a landlord to assign, or transfer, an apartment lease to another financially qualified tenant. We decided to bring a lawsuit to compel the landlord to transfer that apartment lease to me.

He asked me to prepare all of the necessary court papers, but he wanted to draft his own affidavit. He made no other requests. I was shocked, since most tenants in a similar position would have asked for a fortune to cooperate in this lease transfer; this apartment was that unique. He wasn't asking for a penny.

There's no question that he was a special person, even beyond his obvious generosity. I think he sensed my enthusiasm for the place and, on a certain energy level, wanted to help me get it. I've always believed that things and experiences belong to those who can truly appreciate them. After all, if these things and experiences were not available for true enjoyment, why would they even exist? I've always laughed when people drive convertibles with the top up on a perfect day. Why own something if you won't fully enjoy it? I was ready to enjoy this apartment to the nth degree.

I couldn't get the prize out of my mind as I put together the extensive court papers. I completed them and brought the landlord to court.

The first hearing was set for June 27th, a very important date as you will see below.

When the case was first called on the 27th, the landlord's attorney made an application for an adjournment to after July 4th. I introduced myself to that attorney, and suggested we step outside the courtroom to discuss the case. I urged that we resolve this issue on the second call of the court calendar, and he agreed.

I told him I was hoping to move before July 4th and wanted to use the holiday to settle in, so I insisted we try to resolve it that day — June 27th. We discussed the case law, and I advised him that the cases had been coming down in my favor. I reiterated that New York State's highest court (the Court of Appeals) had affirmed a tenant's right to compel a landlord to assign a residential lease to another financially able tenant.

While discussing the case, we discovered that we had a mutual acquaintance — not a huge connection but a connection nonetheless. Several minutes later, the landlord's attorney reluctantly agreed that the case law was in my favor, and consented to execute settlement papers that same day to give me the apartment. I was overjoyed. After resolving a few minor glitches, we signed the settlement documents that same day.

I then met my brother to drink champagne and celebrate at a great outdoor café on Madison Avenue, one of the more joyous spots in Manhattan and perfect for this occasion. Just as I had told the lawyer, I made preparations to move to the new apartment the next week. It was helpful to have that week off to unpack and paint.

When I returned to my office the following week, I received an interesting surprise. On the first page of the *New York Law Journal* was a big story: GOVERNOR SIGNS LAW OUTLAWING ASSIGNMENTS IN RESIDENTIAL LEASES. The new law took effect July 1st, just three days after the landlord agreed to give me that new apartment. There had been a lot of pressure on the New York legislature to rectify what was thought to be an unfair infringement of landlords' rights. The legislature outlawed the expanded rights the Court of Appeals had granted tenants, such as myself, to force the landlord to assign residential leases from one tenant to another. I was unaware that there had been a movement afoot to eliminate this right that had evolved under case law. Had I waited until after July 4th to resolve my lawsuit, as the other attorney wished, I would have lost the lawsuit and the new apartment.

Close call or not, I moved in. For a while, I would wake up in the morning and not really believe I lived there. When I went out on the terrace and gazed across Manhattan, I felt an indescribable rush of positive energy. I have lived in that apartment ever since, and it still feels that way when I survey the incredible view, which has remained largely intact despite a building boom.

I grow herbs and vegetables on that open terrace, including three varieties of tomatoes, eggplant, mild jalapeño peppers, summer squash, mint, basil, rosemary and chives. It's an amazing feeling to watch my plants grow, and then pick fresh produce in the middle of Manhattan.

For so many other reasons, this apartment remains a fresh experience and never ceases to provide a surge of good feelings. This is especially true when I think about the way I got it, and from whom. The fact that I was able to utilize the landlord's negative energy to my benefit made it a sweet result indeed.

When you harness other people's negative energy for your own financial benefit, you will appreciate what I'm talking about. You really feel the experience, the results come from much purer energy, and whatever you acquire seems to have an enduring luster and almost magical protection. If you don't abuse the results, the joy can last indefinitely.

Other people's negative energy can be used to propel you toward greater wealth, as long as you weren't instrumental in causing that negative energy, and provided that you don't react angrily when it is targeted at you. This is a delicate process that requires great awareness on your part, but it can yield impressive results when you gain an energy advantage; the playing field tilts in your favor.

- Recognize negative energy directed at you.
- Understand how and when you have the energy advantage.
- Convert that energy to a financial benefit for you.
- Enjoy the results to the maximum.

CHAPTER 9

INSTANT KARMA AND MONEY

Consider this chapter along with the previous one to understand why others' negative behavior can only harm them while it creates opportunities for you. "Instant karma" is a huge influence in life and in the money making process, so it is crucial to understand how it works. In its simplest form, instant karma refers to the principle of energy that what you put out will come back to you. The tricky part is how and when it comes back — it often returns in a changed form and on its own schedule.

When you understand instant karma, you can develop immunity to others' negative actions, and feel protected in every situation. John Lennon sang:

Instant Karma's gonna get you
Gonna look you right in the face
Better get yourself together darlin'
Join the human race

I thought those lyrics were profound even before I understood their meaning.

When you see your life's events from an energy standpoint, definite patterns of instant karma emerge, and you'll begin to view this knowledge as priceless. When people go out of their way to behave offensively or cause harm without provocation, bad things happen to them and not to you. Of course, this only occurs when you don't take anything personally — and that means not exploding with anger, which is often a conditioned first response.

I began to warn people about this when they dumped negative energy on me. I didn't tell them that Uncle Vinny would go after them with a baseball bat. I simply stated that they should not bother trying to harm me because they would get hurt. Most people laughed when I said that, but I was serious.

The converse of this principle is also true. If I manipulate or control others in a negative way for my own gain, I will get hurt or something will stop me. My karma is so instant now that if I were to physically hit someone without provocation (not that I'd ever do that), someone will raise a hand to me within a short time.

These principles of instant karma apply to everyone, including you. You may have been too busy to notice, you may not be familiar with this concept, or you may not believe in this at all; *it affects you anyway.*

As awareness of instant karma increases, the time it takes for your actions to come back decreases dramatically. If you are skeptical about instant karma, if you think you know so many people who have benefited by lying, cheating, and manipulating, consider this: you are not in those people's skins, and you could never know how they really feel. Those same people are often caught in endless lawsuits over their gains, or strange things happen that prevent them from enjoying any of it. You also have no idea what their experiences have meant to them, or whether or not their lives were improved by their financial gain or the flashiness of their lifestyles. If things are so great, why do so many wealthy people need to numb themselves by abusing drugs or alcohol? Beware of the delusion that fame or money, by itself, protects you from unpleasant or bad things — neither is a shield from the natural forces of karma.

One of my objectives for this book is to help you meet your financial goals with a minimum of disruption to yourself and others. The goal is even loftier — to promote a moneymaking process that's enjoyable to you and to all those you encounter. You will recognize the importance of instant karma as your moneymaking efforts evolve with this process.

Instant karma has become a huge force in my business life. When I first started in the real estate business, I found a promising property in a developing Brooklyn neighborhood. The listing real estate broker loved to give unsolicited advice, and he considered himself quite savvy. I also think he wanted to buy the property he was selling me, but wasn't able to. When I returned to show the property to my construction associate, the broker was there and he overheard our conversation. He called me later and tried to convince me that my contractor didn't know what he was talking about. He claimed that the property needed tens of thousands of dollars' more work than my construction professional had suggested, and that I was foolish to think my associate had estimated the costs correctly. He tried to convince me that I would lose money on the deal, which amounted to extreme negativity on his part.

I listened to what he had to say, and then I ended the conversation. I thought about it for a few minutes and called him back. I told that broker what I thought about his unsolicited opinions in a way I'm sure he didn't forget. But I still had to decide what to do with the property.

I kept hitting a brick wall, and then looked at it from an energy perspective. I thought back on all the times when other people had tried to tell me what I couldn't do; that same negative energy was present. I asked myself if those people were right with their fear-inspiring comments, and they hadn't been. I didn't think they were in tune with my situation. My decision was made, and I went ahead with the transaction. My construction associate renovated the property, and the costs were almost exactly what he projected. The broker had been dead wrong.

I wanted to renovate this property in order to sell it immediately, so I listed it for sale as soon as I signed the contract. I went to contract with a buyer to purchase it before I even closed on it myself. My real estate broker, a very pleasant woman in her mid-fifties, was amazed at this timing and told me, "I can't believe how good your karma was." I agreed with her that my karma was fairly immediate, and very good in that situation. The other real estate broker's interference was malicious, and that gave me an extra boost toward my goal.

The decision to proceed with this transaction was important for other reasons. It taught me to trust my instincts and not someone else's, and it gave me the confidence to try something much bigger and more lucrative in the future.

A poignant example of instant karma occurred several years ago when I sold a beautiful loft in Manhattan's East Village to the tenant who had rented it from me for two years. We became friends during his tenancy, and it seemed natural to sell it to him — and by not using a real estate broker, I passed the savings on to him. Although we were friends, I advised him to hire a lawyer for representation. From my phone dealings with his attorney, I could tell he was a stressed out, obnoxious, and contentious type I had often encountered. One phone conversation stuck in my mind when he found out the purchase price, and made a sarcastic comment: "Oh, I hope you're making a lot of money on this deal."

He sounded resentful; it was obvious that his true feelings were the opposite. Perhaps he, like many attorneys, hated what he did, but had failed to make the effort to leave the legal profession like I had. Nonetheless, it was none of his business how much money I was making, and he was out of line to even mention it. I proceeded carefully and was confident the sale would conclude. It was a straightforward transaction and the buyer, a tech innovator, easily qualified for a mortgage.

The closing took place at his attorney's office. The buyer sat next to me at the closing, and because we were friends;, he didn't follow the custom of sitting next to his attorney. Everything proceeded smoothly except for one glitch the title closer brought up at the end. I owed the buyer approximately sixty-eight dollars due to an unpaid assessment, and when I offered to write a personal, uncertified check for this small amount, the buyer's lawyer immediately objected and insisted on certified funds or cash.

I had almost no cash with me because the closing was early in the morning, and I had anticipated going to the bank *after* the closing with a check for several hundred thousand dollars. I couldn't believe this pettiness designed only to make extra, unnecessary effort for me. I had experienced this type of mindless game playing with many attorneys, one of the many reasons I decided to stop practicing law.

To do as he wanted, I would have to leave the closing, find a cash machine, and come back. This attorney was enjoying the prospect of exercising this small power over me. If he couldn't prevent me from making a lot of money, at least he could inconvenience me a bit. The buyer sensed that his lawyer was being malicious and unreasonable.

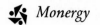

Even the title closer looked up from his paperwork. His expression said it all: the attorney was making things difficult for sport.

I needn't have worried. In one of the quickest examples of instant karma I have ever seen, the title closer hung up the phone and announced that I had paid a tax through the end of the year, and now the buyer owed *me* an adjustment, not the other way around. I have never felt so totally protected, but you should have seen the look on the other attorney's face. I must have spoiled his fun for that day! Being a gracious fellow, I accepted that adjustment of several hundred dollars in an uncertified attorney's check.

Remember that proposed condo conversion in my building? Several interesting examples of instant karma occurred during that two-year process. I will never forget one meeting of the steering committee that took place before we switched attorneys, because the atmosphere was filled with abundant suspicion and drama. The meeting was held in a committee member's apartment, and out of ignorance and fear, she attacked me voraciously because I insisted that we change attorneys. She accused me of being motivated by a kickback. Her attacks were personal, nasty, and paranoid. Her comments could not have been farther from the truth, so I responded with some type of insult, and abruptly left that meeting. In one of the most vivid examples of negativity boomeranging, her apartment caught fire a week later, an unanticipated tragedy of course.

Another tenant suffered a different but more serious fate. One issue that arose during the conversion process was whether tenants should sign a no-buy pledge, an agreement binding all tenants together in their negotiations with the landlord. A no-buy pledge is supposed to provide a united front against the landlord to obtain a better deal. This was a more important issue in other buildings where the landlord was actually negotiating with the tenants. There were no good faith negotiations in our building, so having a no-buy pledge would have been useless. However, I was expected to sign the no-buy pledge since I was on the steering committee.

I had refused to sign it for some time since it was irrelevant, and I didn't want to throw my fate in with people I thought were so uninformed. I was not harming anyone by refusing to sign the no-buy pledge, but periodically, other steering committee members raised it as an issue. They were oblivious to how we were being sold down the river by our existing attorney, and they preferred to expend their energy on this junk.

I received an unsolicited visit one night from a particular tenant enlisted by the steering committee to harass me into signing the no-buy pledge. He was a typical foot soldier with no mind of his own, and was obviously being used by others. He started to argue with me in an extremely offensive manner — and all over nothing, since it wouldn't matter whether I, or anyone else, signed that pledge. My neighbor was convinced he was doing the right thing, but to me he was just following orders. He was a zealot — solemn, joyless, and dangerous to himself and others.

I signed the no-buy pledge under protest several weeks later because, otherwise, I was going to be removed from the steering committee — and I couldn't let that happen because we had not yet changed attorneys. But back to our zealot––I came home from work a few weeks later to find a big crowd in the lobby. Our zealot had taken his own life by shooting himself in the head. His negative energy came back to him in a way no one could have predicted.

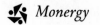

I'd be mortified to think that such extreme karmic repercussions were the result of the bullying or name-calling on the part of these two tenants, but it's reasonable to assume they had treated many other people with the same offensive, negative, and abusive style. I'm not pleased to see either of them so severely punished, but it's difficult not to suspect that their negative actions had negative consequences.

I witnessed powerful effects of instant karma at work, too. I handled cases in landlord-tenant court when I was in-house counsel to a Manhattan real estate firm. One particular judge could only be described as an animal; he routinely screamed at everyone with a malice that exceeded all limits. Yet people accepted it, and most attorneys said nothing out of fear of retribution. Devastating consequences in history have followed people's silence when confronted with unspeakable abuse or injustice, and I was not going to add to that list.

My company had one politically charged case before that judge, and he abused me terribly when I got up to argue my case before him. I continued talking over his ranting and raving, which only infuriated him more. He jumped up from the bench, claimed that I had violated some code of attorney conduct, ran out of the courtroom like a raving lunatic, then came back two minutes later and threatened to file charges against me — an obvious attempt to punish me for standing up to him.

He was even too cowardly to decide the case, which involved a woman who had stayed in her apartment for eighteen months without paying any rent, which is not so unusual in the politicized world of New York City real estate. He remanded that case for further action by another judge. I completely forgot about his threats until about six months later, when I received a notice of his complaint against me with the bar association disciplinary committee. At that point, I no longer worked for the same real estate company, as I had decided to practice law on my own and pursue the real estate business. I answered the complaint myself, and was convinced that the disciplinary committee would throw it out. I filed my opposition papers, but was surprised that I lost at the first level of administrative review. Although it was a minor blemish, I thought the decision was unjustified. I appealed the decision and requested a hearing in person.

I decided not to appeal alone. I called my former employer and told him what happened. He was extremely active in a Manhattan real estate trade organization, and enlisted its help to defend me. Since this judge had been continually abusive to so many people, this trade organization was looking for an opportunity to expose what that judge was about. They were also looking for someone — like me — who wasn't afraid of the judge. They hired one of the top real estate law firms in New York to defend me. I had my own two-member dream team defense, and one of my lawyers wrote a respected column in a prominent legal newspaper, so most judges didn't want to get on his bad side.

I wish you could have seen the look on that judge's face when I arrived at the hearing for the appeal, and he saw who was defending me. He had probably thought I was just a young lawyer with no connections, and he could push me around without consequence. As my lawyer cross-examined him, a nice turn of events, he fidgeted and squirmed. He was on the defensive, not me.

The hearing lasted about two hours, but it took the appeals board exactly five minutes to dismiss all charges against me.

That's not the only thing that happened. This hearing occurred about the same time that I had started to take acting classes to break out of my mold. I had just sent my headshot to an agent, and she booked me for a photo shoot the next day with a national magazine at a New Jersey estate. It was a totally joyful experience and the polar opposite from the disciplinary committee hearing.

In another example of instant karma, that same judge resigned in disgrace within a short time, and was no longer in a position to abuse people. When you try to destroy someone else for no reason, the only one who gets destroyed is you.

Instant karma is a huge energy force in the universe. Become familiar with its workings if you want to increase your wealth, and have a peaceful and happy life. Don't doubt its impact because the external life of someone you observe to be malicious seems unaffected. You never really know how someone else is feeling, whether they can sleep at night, what drugs they need to take to cope, etc. It is fascinating to experience the interplay between instant karma and converting negative energy to money; use it to produce your own financial windfall.

- Understand how instant karma works alone and with the conversion of negative energy.
- Recognize instant karma as a real force in your life.
- Observe how instant karma affects your moneymaking process.
- Adjust your behavior to produce the best karma.
- When you realize that other people's actions produce their own consequences, you can stop wasting your energy on revenge and retribution. Leave that up to the universe and move on with your prosperity plans.

CHAPTER 10

YOUR ENERGY SPHERE OF INFLUENCE

Your "energy sphere of influence" is a snapshot of who you are in this moment. It is shaped by your birth, upbringing, choice of education, mate and other factors. You absorb different energy from all those sources, and then filter that energy through your own unique nature and physiognomy. The energies you absorb through these experiences and the resulting opportunities that become available to you constitute your energy sphere of influence. Your effectiveness and ultimate happiness in each moment is determined by the interplay between your own energy sphere and that of others. Your immune system and consciousness determine the energies that are absorbed or blocked as you move through each day.

Your energy sphere is not a static thing, since you absorb an abundance of energy each moment. The "energy sphere of influence" refers to the sum total of things available to you immediately or within a very short time frame, not to opportunities contingent on future events.

We live in a time of unprecedented political, economic, and social change: wars that seem to never end with large groups of people migrating, income disparity accelerating, and new technologies appearing overnight. These changes can be frightening to some who think the world is imploding, or you can embrace these accelerated shifts as creating fresh opportunities in your energy sphere. *It's your choice.* Thinking about your energy sphere in this manner permits you to custom design your financial world as never before, by identifying and then building upon your own uniqueness. This may not be easy, but it can be very rewarding. Experiment with different combinations until you find what is right for you. Look for things that make your spirit soar — the purer the better. And those things may change over time, because every endeavor and relationship has a certain cycle. Appraise new opportunities through the conscious prism of your own nature. And while you do this, re-discover your natural innocence, trust your inner sense, and enjoy every step of the way.

Since your energy sphere of influence is in flux, windows of opportunity need to be considered, or a situation may pass or radically change. When I first entered the real estate business, I looked at properties in neighborhoods that were considered undesirable. I thought I had unlimited time to decide what properties to buy. I bought one building from a group of foreclosed properties, but I was strongly interested in a second property, a beautiful brownstone in a marginal area. The process of buying the first property was a stretch in so many ways, so I was hesitant about the second property. Unbeknownst to me, the market for properties in those areas was changing fast. In the several months it took me to decide to purchase the second property, the price doubled and it rose out of my reach. Today, that same property is worth more than ten times the price originally offered to me.

I learned an important lesson from this experience: You can be sure there are other people working toward the same goals as you, and every opportunity is a vacuum that the universe quickly fills. When something comes close to or within reach of your energy sphere, have the wherewithal to grasp it. Stretch to reach it if necessary, but don't let it pass you by.

Understanding how the components of your energy sphere interact is important. If you work in advertising but become unhappy and wish to change fields, you might try things that have some relationship to advertising, such as marketing, consulting, or writing. If you want to try something totally different, that might be terrific too, provided the new field bears some relationship to a personal passion, interest, or field of study. If you just woke up one day and decided to become a nuclear physicist, but had never taken physics in school and hated mathematics, this would not be a good change. That wish, that desire, would not be within your energy sphere of influence, and pursuing it would be a huge mistake. If you made those changes anyway, you would certainly fail, and not just because you had been deluding yourself.

On the other hand, if you decided to leave that advertising job and open a dance studio, this could be within your energy sphere of influence if you had always loved dancing, had taken dance classes, and had always dreamed about working with dancers. If you had that same love of dancing, but had a bad foot that sporadically gave you acute pain, opening that dance studio would not be the wisest course. Similarly, if you were an accountant who dreamed of a more adventurous life, you might try leading safaris in Africa. However, if you had severe allergies triggered by the outdoors, leaving the accounting job to lead safaris would go against your physical constitution and prove disastrous.

While these examples may seem obvious, they illustrate basic elements of an energy sphere of influence. The choices you make usually contain subtle factors that need to be considered. I intuitively found practicing law repugnant, yet it took me awhile to decipher why. I eventually realized that contentiousness goes against my nature and depresses my spirit. I disliked being saddled with weighty problems at a young age when I would have preferred to be exploring the world, or working at something fun. This was no reflection on my level of compassion for other people, but it was my reaction to having their problems constantly dumped on my shoulders — even for pay. Many of those problems were created out of stupidity or greed. I discovered that my spirit soared when I was involved with something more constructive, creative, and positive, like acting. Real estate development also fulfilled my needs in a big way, because people enjoyed what I created and I could see tangible results over time.

Other people's evaluations of my strengths kept me stuck in the legal profession too long. I seemed to be doing "just fine" to them, but I knew better. Only after I honestly appraised my own nature was I able to shift out of law. The closer I got to my nature, the better my access was to all the right energy I needed to reconfigure my financial world.

This sounds great if you have a true sense of what direction to go in to achieve your financial goals, but what if you don't have a clue? Even if you can't define your energy sphere of influence *yet,* you can identify situations and things you hate or strongly dislike. A good first step is to eliminate those things from your life. As you get more and more confident about letting go of things that don't work, you'll consider opportunities in a new light, with your eyes wide open and mindful of your energy sphere. Always listen to that little voice inside you. Even if the results aren't perfect, you gain experiences you were meant to learn from.

Many people are afraid to let go of what they have until something new and better has materialized. They use the same rationale to hold on to bad personal relationships. When something is causing such discomfort, it is sometimes better to just let go to make room for something new. Be poised to experience what everyone seems afraid of — a time period when you have nothing, and you just exist or be. The benefit of this stage is rarely acknowledged, but is actually quite considerable: you may not have what you want yet, but you will no longer be in a bad situation or relationship, and you will have created the space — an energy void — for what you want to manifest.

I made a conscious decision to turn away certain legal cases while making the transition to the real estate business. Some people couldn't understand why I would do that and thought it treasonous. I was told that I was crazy, that all business is alike, and that I was missing out on all kinds of financial gain. I didn't care, because I knew how awful I felt when I accepted those kinds of cases. I also knew, given my nature and constitution, that I wouldn't have survived in good form had I followed their advice. It was liberating for me to say "no" to certain clients, knowing how uncomfortable I would have been had I accepted their work.

As you look at your life with more honesty and become aware of the particular qualities, experiences, and nature that make you unique, examine the people you surround yourself with and consider how they affect your energy sphere. The more exposure you have to these people, the more you will absorb their energy. A recent Internet study revealed that your state of mind, including whether you are happy or depressed, is closely linked to the emotional states of your three closest friends. Choose those friends carefully.

This book is not about energy and healing per se, but all energy is related, whether directed to financial or physical health. Thus, the quality of energy necessary to protect your energy sphere of influence in financial matters is the same quality of energy necessary to protect your physical health and the way you age. A great deal of physical and mental illness is caused by repeated absorption of the wrong type of energy. Often, the energy that precedes a physical "dis-ease" is a traumatic emotional event occurring in your energy field. The absorption of this emotional imbalance lands in the body as a last resort. If that energy accumulates and is not released, it wreaks havoc with your immune system and your physical health. It affects different parts of your body, depending upon your particular genetic makeup and environmental factors. Most major diseases, or so-called accidents (there are none, by the way) are just wake-up calls for you to assess your life — forced time-out periods. It is the rare individual who voluntarily takes time out when major change is necessary, or who stops behavior when it doesn't feel right.

If you don't heed the call to re-evaluate your life, wake-up calls will continue until you stop whatever you've been doing — or die. The best health insurance is provided by your own actions, especially whether you remain in a reactive state, or learn how to watch events for what they can teach you, without emotional turmoil. If you do the right thing every minute of the day, if you are constantly aware and monitor your energy, if you learn how to release harmful emotional energy that occurs in your sphere, you will have no need to get sick. This is a process, so don't be deterred if it doesn't happen at once. It also represents the pinnacle of human existence and is best looked at as a goal.

In periods of risk, I was very careful about the people I allowed access to me. I made this effort to protect my energy sphere. I was aware that I needed all of my life energy to achieve my goals, and that the energy I needed to access was very subtle. However, we all have relationships that can be messy and/or complicated. During this time, I requested that certain people stay away from me; I was at a critical point in a real estate project. I made the request as nicely as I could, fully aware that I didn't have the luxury of being distracted by their energy. Asking this from the people in your life may or may not be a viable option.

I can only speculate that my convictions were being tested, because my requests were not honored. Since I wasn't left alone, I reacted emotionally and exploded at these people (something I hope would never occur today). It sucked me into the trap I had wanted to avoid all along, and then I had no choice but to ride out this negative intrusion into my energy sphere.

I tried to remember my own advice regarding turning other people's negative energy to my own gain. It was some consolation that I was prescient about this intrusion and took steps to avoid it, even though my efforts didn't work. However, there were impressive lessons to be learned from my own triggered negative energy. For one thing, I was amazed to witness how the fallout in my life was immediate. It really was *instant* karma. At the time, I was negotiating with a commercial tenant for my project and was 99 percent sure the negotiations would conclude favorably.

After this intrusion in my energy sphere and my angry emotional response, the prospective tenant backed away overnight. This wasn't the only immediate effect. What I thought would be a routine certification by local government authorities turned into a nightmare of extra inspections that took three or four more weeks. These additional three or four weeks before I received a final Certificate of Occupancy (C of O) put me in a bind because I had a tight deadline to conclude the financing with my bank.

I remember sitting in the government office responsible for giving the final C of O, which was supposed to be generated after four related governmental sections conducted their own set of inspections. The actual inspections were completed and the building passed, but my architect said the final C of O was sometimes received weeks, if not months, after the inspections were done; it was just a bureaucratic thing. I didn't have those extra weeks because the inspections had taken four weeks longer than initially planned and my bank was breathing down my neck to close.

Faced with a deadline that could destroy my project, I did what I customarily do when people impose limitations upon me: I took matters into my own hands and tried to break through. Yes, I would be doing the architect's job, but what he had told me about the wait was *unacceptable*. I went down to my architect's office, took the building file, and went to the New York City Department of Buildings. My goal was to go to each of the four sections of the Building Department that had inspected my building (plumbing, electrical, heating, etc.), and insist that the approval be entered in each of their computers. After this was accomplished, the C of O could be generated for the whole building. My architect said I was crazy and it could not be done, because things didn't work that way. I didn't care about his warning, because I had no choice; there wasn't any way I couldn't get it done that day.

I don't know whether you've ever needed something quickly from your local government, or done business with any building department where you live, but even though it is often in the news due to general corruption, the NYC Building Department is a lot better than it used to be. On my way down to its downtown Brooklyn office, I decided to take the most pragmatic approach possible. I knew I couldn't react angrily to anything said or done by its employees, since that would be a death blow to getting the C of O.

Armed with that mindset, I went to the Building Department on that Friday morning and was one of the first to enter. It took me about two hours to get the first section's approval. I then went to the next section, and was met with bureaucratic indifference. It was as though time had stopped in this section and no one was in a hurry to do anything.

I had anticipated encountering this, so I decided I wasn't going to get angry or show an attitude. I wasn't going to give these people any extra reason to torture me. I grabbed a seat and started to meditate. I never let go of my goal in my mind, and I acted as relaxed as someone on vacation. I would periodically get up from my seat, and politely inquire if someone would give me their section's approval before lunch. I was unbelievably nice in the face of this indifference, and I never pushed it. It worked. I got approval from the second of four sections before lunch. When I dashed out for a quick lunch at 1:00 PM, I actually had a glimmer of hope that I could pull this off. Nevertheless, I made extra efforts to stay vigilant because I didn't want to be complacent. If I became lax or projected too much enthusiasm, it would be deadly for me in the afternoon. I got back to the Building Department at 1:30 PM, hoping someone in the third section might return early from lunch. I was lucky and someone opened the door at 1:45 pm. I walked right in. This employee was actually nice and seemed competent, too, so I made a judgment call and went out on a limb. I told him that I absolutely needed his approval that same day. I emphasized that if I didn't get it, the financing for my building would fall through. I would never have taken this tack with an employee who appeared hostile.

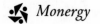

It worked. He told me to come back to his office by 3:00 PM for the third section's approval, and he kept his word. I was beginning to feel a little elated, but I couldn't let it out yet. I still had the fourth section's approval to get, and as I entered that fourth section's office my heart sank. The office had the feeling of a morgue where things moved very slowly. I needed a different tactic here, so I made a withdrawal from my charm bank. *Boy oh boy,* I thought to myself. *It had better be a big withdrawal, considering whom I have to charm!* I wanted to act nonchalant, and pay as many compliments to as many people as possible. I tried to create a good and fun energy around me, which helped me forget that this was a very important event in my life. If I couldn't get all four approvals on that day, my goose was cooked.

The gods must have been with me because at exactly 4:27 PM, I received the fourth section's approval. The final C of O for the building was generated at 4:45 PM, and I actually got to hold it in my hands. I was emotionally and physically drained, but also thrilled. I knew the final roadblock in this difficult but incredibly stretching project had been cleared, and that I could close with my financial institution the next week as required.

When I left the building at 5:00 PM, it hit me — all the chances I had taken and the efforts I made. I called my architect and told him the good news. He was a little speechless, but happy. I just wanted to go home and collapse, but that's not what happened.

As I made my way home from downtown Brooklyn, the real estate broker who was leasing the remaining loft unit for me called. He had potential tenants who had to see that unit in the next hour; they were chefs who were relocating from California to open a new Manhattan restaurant the next week. The broker asked if I could show the unit myself, since he had an emergency to take care of. I made the effort to show that loft even though I was tired. The chefs rented it on the spot.

Not only that. Remember the commercial tenant who backed away after the intrusion into my energy sphere? As soon as I got back from a much-needed vacation after the closing with my bank the following week, I got a call from two brokers who had prospective tenants. A minor bidding war took place for my commercial space, and the commercial tenant I finally got was better than the one I had suddenly lost. Not only did I rent that commercial space for more money, but with this tenant, unlike the one I had lost, there was no need to offer free rent for a build out. This tenant's planned use for the space was more in line with the artistic use I had wanted, since the tenant I had lost was a restaurant.

I had tunneled into a patch of negative energy when I exploded at the people who had punctured my energy sphere. This negative energy had a certain cycle. I was able to move through that cycle and turn it around for my own financial benefit, but it was quite a whirlwind. Those extra inspections by the four sections, with the attending delays and pressure to obtain a final C of O, had taken their toll. Losing that first commercial tenant was really disappointing at the time. However, I really did *feel* these experiences. It was like wrestling with the gods, which is what you should expect when you radically change your financial world. You are ultimately at their mercy, but they love it when you fight back. If you can muster the fortitude to persevere, there's very often a nice bonus tossed in at the end.

Looking back at that completed project, I realized some other things. This was the building I had initially found in such a short time after that former colleague of mine started to withhold legal work, and treat me so malevolently in our shared office space. Once you are comfortable with riding those waves, getting out of the comfort zone, using others' negative energy, and instant karma, along with the other principles mentioned in this book, you will get the opportunities you want. This is the first step. You should be prepared for all the work that comes along with it to bring your dream to fruition. Don't expect an easy ride with any of this, but it will be an interesting and life affirming one.

When you go through several of these cycles and really experience and feel each of them, you will appreciate how your energy sphere really works. You will also witness a gradual transformation within your-self. You will still occupy the same physical body that you did before — you're not magically transported to another planet — but in some very real sense, you are transported to a different place, a different way of viewing things, a change of consciousness about money and life. You are transported to a realm of financial abundance where you have as much control over your financial world as is humanly possible — and that financial change can be sustained if you know how to maintain good opportunities, and when to cycle out. You may find that you have enough money for the foreseeable future and choose to pursue other endeavors. Whatever you do, take some time to savor all the blessings in your energy sphere now.

The clarity with which you see every aspect of your life is greatly enhanced, too, which is a priceless gift you have to earn for yourself. Don't forget the results of your efforts, but don't focus on them too much. Respect the integrity of the process that achieved these great results because you'll want to be able to go back for more.

The game of life is won and lost on a daily basis — on a moment-to-moment basis. Your energy sphere is the playing field. Look for incremental steps and feel each of them, then allow each step to lead you to the next, and feel your power increase. Don't complain, don't explain, and never sell out. To win, you must keep your energy sphere as clean, as pure, and as honest as possible. Be free in your mind and your heart, regardless of your personal responsibilities. Don't let anyone take your lifeblood from you and deplete your energy sphere. Repair any puncture to your sphere as soon as possible, and move on.

Treat everyone who comes across your path as the precious entity they are, even if that other person isn't aware of their own divinity. Surround yourself with people, places, and things that make your spirit soar.

Everything you say and do with anybody is an energy exchange that can enhance or detract from your energy sphere, and affect all those around you. Never underestimate the power of anyone to change your life in a big way. There is no such thing as a casual remark. Every remark carries energy and importance, and has a direct impact on both you and those around you. This is especially true during critical times, when you are riding those waves, because the energy you put out will greatly impact your results. That's instant karma.

A critical tool for maintaining a pure energy sphere is visualization; if you can see it, you can be it. Visualization is the ability to mentally create what you want in your life before it actually occurs by picturing it in your mind. It involves consciously maintaining that image in your mind for ten or fifteen minutes a day (or however long you choose), and doing this until what you want manifests in reality. The way visualization works is a mystery, but by opening your mind and heart this way, it helps you reach your intended goals. Visualization is one of the most powerful tools accessible to each of us. Use it at every available opportunity.

A spiritual visionary who recognized this was the late Neville Goddard, who often spoke of how "imagining creates reality." He wrote many books on this subject, and his works can be found on his website.[4] His theories complement the holographic theory of existence,[5] which suggests there is no one objective reality, but that each of us creates our own reality produced by our own thoughts. If this is true (and I believe it is), one who masters his thoughts is truly master of his domain.

Fear has a huge influence here, too. As the famous spiritual master Osho states in his book *Courage: The Joy of Living Dangerously:* "A fearless person is someone who never creates fear in anybody, and who never allows anybody to create fear in him."

Other factors influence your energy sphere, too. One of the most important is the concept of self-delusion. Each of us needs a dash of self-delusion to stay sane in this world. An example: I give myself the benefit of the doubt most of the time, because I can and no one else will. I may overestimate my abilities a wee bit in situations, but why not? It feels life affirming to me, and I believe it enhances my energy sphere.

But I am aware of when I do this and I don't fool myself. Too many people delude themselves when it comes to major life issues. This will defeat your efforts to develop a new moneymaking process, and will sabotage your real self-worth, too. Fundamental honesty about your abilities, your nature, your likes and dislikes, and even your physiognomy, is essential to maximizing your energy sphere.

Morality, too, has a huge influence on your energy sphere, but the morality you are taught growing up rarely exists in everyday life. Things and people turn out to be not as they should be but as they are, and

4. www.NevilleGoddard.com

5. To learn more, read *The Holographic Universe,* by Michael Talbot.

there's a huge difference between the two. Unrealistic expectations usually lead to disappointment and self-delusion. This doesn't mean there is no appropriate code of behavior or responsibility for you to follow, but you have to fashion it for yourself.

That new morality will include factors your mother was never aware of, and couldn't teach you. Your moral sense should assess the level of malevolence and negativity of the energy in each life situation so you can act accordingly. As you show absolute respect to every person who crosses your path, you also realize there is no obligation to be nice to anyone who wants to control you for their own selfish ends. The unbridled generosity I shower on almost every person and situation in my life can be withdrawn immediately when I detect ingratitude. These are my choices; you need to fashion your own.

With no broken-down morality binding you, you become less attached to the appearance of every facet of your life, and you move toward personal freedom; *you master the priceless art of detachment.* On an energy level, you also become protected and untouchable, because you operate from a place of absolute love and respect, a place few people ever reach. To maintain that level of consciousness, you must remain vigilant.

With every effort you make, in every minute of the day, you build your protection and your morality — a *continuing morality,* or a *movable morality feast.* Traditional morality depends on entrenched and often hypocritical forces telling you how to lead your life — or else you'll go to hell, become a bad person, lose respect, or suffer some other unpleasant fate. The morality you create for yourself is far more life enhancing, and comes with no accompanying threats, judgments, or implied punishment. It puts responsibility right where it belongs — in your hands. It provides you with the tools to deal realistically and effectively with what you are actually going to encounter in this world, rather than in some pie-in-the-sky notion of human behavior and post-mortem reward. It presents you with options, and shows you how to develop your own unlimited access to financial opportunities designed to enhance, rather than destroy, others' lives. Your goal is to gain control over your financial world, not to control or manipulate others, or to boost your ego. *Think of it as access without the usual attachments.*

Many people have so much money, yet are unable to enjoy most of it. Their money can become a burden, or what defines them, as opposed to a force for life enhancement. Many people have so little and are deprived of life's necessities and luxuries. Wouldn't it be nice to actively participate in balancing things out for yourself and others? You can do that and learn to really enjoy all the things on your plate. By changing your own financial access, you simultaneously alter the balance of the "haves" and "have-nots" in a way that benefits everyone.

A prominent executive ran a clothing company with his sister. This executive traveled six months of the year, but not for business — for inspiration. He claimed that such travel tremendously enhanced his effectiveness in business, and I remember thinking how interesting that sounded. It seemed almost too good to be true, but I didn't disbelieve it or think it impossible. It felt like something I could potentially enjoy doing.

Things often don't ring true for me until I experience them myself. *I urge you to personally experience as many of the principles in this book as possible.*

I spend more time traveling now than when I practiced law, and I enjoy the benefits. Travel helps remind me what life is like elsewhere, gets me out of my comfort zone, and keeps me mindful of other people's realities. This system suits my nature better than having constant work obligations with a limited and fixed vacation schedule. After finishing with a time-consuming and draining legal case, I found a mountain of paperwork on my desk — paperwork that involved cleaning up other people's messy problems. The notion of healthy recovery time was absent. My life is completely different today, and a changing variety of techniques keep it that way.

Make a concerted daily effort to protect your energy sphere. Travel to exciting places as often as you can. Spend more time in pleasant surroundings and enjoy the majesty of nature. Set aside enough down-time each day for some form of meditation or physical exercise, or for just doing nothing — your choice. Actively choose work projects based on how the energy feels, not on whether it will guarantee you any result, money included. Turn your whole idea of security on its head and shake it out.

If you make these shifts, you will feel more connected to the flow of energy and to abundance. When people ask how you're doing, they are often referring to your financial status and not to your health. But it won't matter, because you'll be able to honestly answer, "Great!"

When I take a short time-out, I love to drive north of New York City through some of the most beautiful scenery I've ever seen. The drive starts in New York City, then crosses the George Washington Bridge and continues onto the Palisades Parkway, which goes briefly through New Jersey, then back into New York. I've discovered some really beautiful roads surrounded by huge trees that wind along the Hudson River. The energy I absorb from these drives is incredible, particularly if I stop and walk the paths that line the prehistoric cliffs in New Jersey.

On one drive, I experienced something unusual on my ride home. I stopped for coffee at a beautiful outdoor café in a small town perched high over the Hudson River. I decided to make the drive home a different "experience," so I listened to some previously unreleased Jimi Hendrix songs put together by his daughter after his death.

I had heard of the "Summer of Love" in 1968 in the San Francisco Bay area, but was too young to have experienced it myself. On the trip back to Manhattan, the "Jimi Hendrix Experience" and the drive along the water transported me to that time and place in my mind, which was all I really needed. I'm not saying that I actually experienced time travel, but regardless of where I was transported to on that ride, the feelings were great, and those good vibes lasted that whole night and part of the next day.

I've also discovered the wine country on the North Fork of Long Island where more than thirty wineries occupy an incredibly picturesque and non-commercial country setting, just a two-hour drive from Manhattan. If you blink twice, you would swear you are in California.

The absorption of this kind of energy boosts my immune system, my sense of well-being, and my energy sphere. I monitor my energy during these drives, and I notice how it can shift, with many of my preoccupations fading quickly. I feel like a different person when I return because I have connected to great physical beauty and to something outside myself.

Beside these excursions, I find it enormously enhancing to go for hikes in some of the mountain ranges like Bear Mountain north of New York. I love walking, driving or biking anywhere near water, where I am likely to absorb positive energy. I go down to the Hudson River Park in lower Manhattan just to enjoy the spectacular sunsets. It helps if these excursions are undisturbed by electronic distractions. These immersions into or close to nature may seem relatively mundane, but in an age of constant assault by so many unnatural/electronic elements, they help maintain my energy sphere and my sense of humanity. Explore the beautiful natural surroundings accessible to you with your phone off and you will reap similar benefits.

It is illuminating to consider how your energy sphere is constantly changing. The more you discover about it, the better you can shape the future of your finances and the happier you become, because you act from awareness and an authentic morality. You appreciate how to preserve and enhance your energy sphere, and you gladly share your knowledge and benefits with everyone, without being under anyone's control.

- Learn about your energy sphere of influence and honestly appraise its components.
- Turn away tasks you intuitively don't connect with. Leave space in your life for appealing opportunities.
- Fashion your own workable morality.
- Reject fear projected onto you, and never inspire others to be afraid.
- Spend more time in pleasant, inspiring surroundings, and absorb that beautiful energy.
- Visualize goals and dreams to help bring them into reality.

CHAPTER 11

END YOUR LIMITATIONS

We are all born with certain inclinations, and our conditioning puts an additional layer of compulsions and desires upon us — adding up to our sense of self. Like most things in life, this self is not perfect, since it contains a full complement of fears, expectations, and limitations. It is helpful to look at it as some kind of imprint.

End those fears and limitations to create the financial world you want. The good news is that you can make huge dents in your fears and limitations through small and consistent efforts. For every step you take, the release of layers of unwanted energy is palpable; it makes room for the new connections you need. From an energy standpoint, you are reconnecting to who you were before everything was dumped upon you (like a controlling matrix or grid), so that access to your financial goals can be strong and long lasting. You find your original self.

I saw a televised interview with one of the more respected actresses of our time. She seemed intelligent, not because she went to Yale Drama School, but because she was aware of how limitations had been thrust upon her when she was young. She spoke about her experience at Yale Drama School, which had a solid reputation for preparation in the arts, but was also viewed as stodgy and limiting in certain circles. She spoke of one professor who repeatedly told her she had no talent and would be better off not acting. Her comment about the professor was quite telling and heartfelt, because she argued that it wasn't right that any one person should have so much influence over a young person. It isn't right according to what traditional morality says, but it happens all the time. Her professor made a real gash in her emotional armor, which has affected her to this day. Her comments show how susceptible she was to the input of energy, particularly when she was young and less certain of her abilities, and looking to others for guidance. That kind of seepage can occur to anybody at any age. We are like sponges that absorb the energy thrust upon us, unless we are constantly aware.

It would have been a huge loss for our culture if that actress had listened to that professor and stopped acting. She can have the last laugh now, but only because she worked hard to overcome a limitation that was imposed upon her.

We can all relate to this story. I'm sure somebody tried to derail you during your formative years, or later in life. These limitations and fears were dumped on you because you were in the sphere of that critical person. You absorb that energy and think it is "you," but it never really is. These negative energy dumpers can be teachers, parents, relatives, friends, acquaintances, employers, coworkers, or strangers. The limitations and fears they impart often become lifetime partners in preventing you from reaching your potential, or they cripple you emotionally, or both. These gifts keeps on giving until you decide to throw the limitations off, get down to core, and expand to become who you want.

I once believed it was important to have a mentor for my development. This belief set me up for some unhealthy dependencies, general disappointment, and a huge fall — because the idea of a single mentor is fundamentally flawed. The notion that someone older and more experienced would be willing, let alone able, to impart his or her wisdom or accumulated experiences to me turned out to be a delusion. I ultimately found I had the wisdom and knowledge within me for any endeavor. You may not have been brought up to believe it, but you can accomplish anything without someone "older and wiser" leading the way.

Knowledge or experience does not belong to any one person, even though many people assume otherwise. You can learn something from every personal and work-related life experience. Work with other people toward common goals, and respect each person's abilities and knowledge for a good collaboration. It isn't productive to feel inferior to anyone who has a particular work experience that you don't.

I worked with three or four mentors when I was in my twenties and early thirties. I was eager to work closely with each of them and to absorb the benefits of their experience. I thought I needed them if I was to excel at what I did and create the financial world I wanted.

After working with them, I began to notice some cracks in their armor. They turned out to be flawed human beings — just like the rest of us. Each of them was intelligent, successful in the traditional sense, and had earned a certain respect, but working closely with them gave me a different lens through which to view their actions and their success. Although many people would automatically view them as moral because of their supposed status, I found their actions to be anything but moral — another reason why each of us should construct our own notion of morality. Each of them was ruled strongly by ego, was proud of goals they'd reached, and saw his knowledge as a kind of possession he had uniquely developed. They exhibited a strong element of control in their actions toward me. Their so-called specialized knowledge and expertise was doled out ever so slowly to prevent me from eclipsing them, as though there was an ongoing contest.

The only person with whom you are truly in a contest with is you — that is the person you are challenging yourself to become. I knew I didn't want to be controlled by anybody. I didn't think being controlled or put in my place should be a precondition of acquiring knowledge of any kind. Until I learned how to tap into the knowledge myself, I thought it would be a mistake to stop working with those mentors.

Each of these mentors had a substantial reverence for money and success. I tried not to absorb this energy, but it was all around me: I breathed it in like noxious fumes. Ironically, I needed to let go of that reverence for money before I could develop and tap into my own prosperity consciousness.

I recall a mentor I had in a real estate company who asked for my advice on a particular transaction. He was one of those Yale graduates who had achieved success in the traditional sense, and he was always trying to lord his money over me. He thought his money would impress me because I was younger than he was — he thought I was *less rich*. I was impressed with some of his accomplishments, but only to a point. When I saw that his personal life was empty and soulless, my opinion of him changed, and I saw the real limits of money as a goal unto itself.

He went into contract to buy a group of buildings when someone offered him a million dollar profit just to flip, or sell, the contract. He asked me what I would do in his situation. I told him that one million dollars sounded pretty good to me, and I suggested he take the offer. He thought it wasn't *enough* money; he wanted $100,000 more. I even heard him brag about this offer to his business friends on the phone. When that potential purchaser set up a meeting to take over the contract, he told the purchaser that he wanted that extra $100,000. The purchaser agreed to pay this premium on the phone, but never showed up at the meeting to buy the contract. My boss frantically called the purchaser several times, but he never responded because he was no longer interested in buying those buildings *at any price*. Unbeknownst to my employer, the market for that property was beginning to turn downward. Since my boss thought he was so smart, he couldn't understand why he hadn't sensed the market turndown. Can you identify the problems he faced? They are our old friends ego and greed — the two things that bring most people down, and that certainly play a role in most economic meltdowns.

My boss got stuck with these buildings, and he had lots of trouble just closing the transaction. That was only the beginning. Managing those properties was difficult and caused him substantial aggravation, and it added substantially to my workload. He used to say that all that aggravation was causing him to "pull the hair right out of his head." I thought this was funny, because most of the hair on his head was in a toupee. I promised myself one thing while watching this fiasco: if someone ever offered me one million dollars just to flip a contract, I'd take it!

It feels great not to work for other people anymore. Not that I didn't learn things from those experiences, but the whole idea of needing another individual as a mentor has been destroyed in my mind. *Life experience, available to everyone 24/7, is the ultimate mentor.* Once I was able to cultivate my own strengths and not revere others, I was in a position to move ahead, without anyone constantly trying to keep me in my place — and without any limitations other than those I placed on myself.

Begin to see the world through your own limitations and not those of others. Once those limitations are clear, break them down one by one. Expand your notion of what's possible in every moment of your life. Every step changes the energy around you, and makes you more receptive to possible opportunities. It could start with something simple, such as extending your daily walk a small amount, or working just a little harder at the gym. When you identify, access, and then follow through on just one experience, you feel your own expanding power, which becomes a mental building block for other activities, including changes to your financial world. You become familiar with and accustomed to breaking down limitations on a daily basis in whatever you do. Thus, you cultivate a mental and physical ability to recognize and take advantage of unfolding opportunity.

Breaking down limitations in your life can sometimes mean giving yourself permission to do nothing, when you might otherwise have reacted in a mechanical way. Remember the will contest in chapter 1, when sitting in that courtroom and meditating was the most effective thing to do? It was important to be prepared for the court case, but it was not necessary to be agitated. Meditating helped me remain calm while waiting for the case to be called, which was the perfect energy for winning it.

We are conditioned to react in a certain way when others irritate us or make us feel threatened. Attempt a different approach when someone says or does something that makes you uncomfortable. Instead of reacting in a hurtful or angry way, see the perceived assault as an opportunity to expand your experience on the emotional plane. Once you can detach and accomplish this, you become enriched by behavior that previously drove you crazy. It becomes a precious gift.

There are other benefits to living with a mindset of constant expansion. You avoid becoming self-satisfied, and you create a life that is always evolving regardless of your age. You become an instrument of change in whatever you do, and an example of personal freedom for all.

When you constantly prove that you can push the envelope, even by the simplest of means, your energy will lead you to the opportunities you need. Once these opportunities become available, you can take advantage of them wholeheartedly without holding back. Enjoy them until they run their cycle, however long that is. Your lack of complacency prepares you for the next round of opportunities and connects you to what you need. You become the master of your own fate.

Everyone accumulates limitations from different family backgrounds, life experiences, and conditioning. Those limitations are beliefs that must be discarded before you can develop wealth through this process. Becoming present and aware in every moment is a great tool for dissolving those limitations, especially when you realize that nobody but you has the key to unlock your riches. There may be those who appear farther along than you in accessing wealth, but that is mostly illusion, and should not stop you from developing at your own speed, eliminating limitations, and enjoying every step of the process.

- Appraise and eliminate unwanted limitations imposed on your life.
- Seek the counsel of those more skilled and experienced than you, but don't put them on a pedestal, or think you can't succeed without them.
- Focus on present moment awareness, expand your idea of what is possible in every moment, and use this consciousness to create wealth.

PART IV

ENERGY EVOLUTION

Chapter 12

Tap Into the Source

The source" is not a place where you can physically go to, but it is a place nonetheless. And there are definite ways to access it. The source exists in your mind, in my mind, and in everybody's mind, and it has always existed.

It makes perfect sense that all knowledge and human experience that has ever occurred exists within you on a certain level in its purest and most powerful form. It makes sense because no one person should be able to possess any knowledge, information, or experience just for himself. Knowledge belongs to us all. You just need to learn how to tap into it.

The existence of the source makes sense on a scientific basis, too, because all humans come from the same place and possess the same genetic coding. Genetic coding is nothing more than the cumulative body of learned and acquired information that has ever existed. It is, on a cellular level, the cumulative experience of mankind being passed on from generation to generation. Compare the source to the Internet: I'm sure that few people could have imagined anything like the Internet's scope and influence just twenty years ago. We now access the Internet every day for so many of our needs. The source has similarities to the Internet in terms of the wealth of knowledge and information available, but the source is purer, richer, deeper, and more complete, with a lot less pornography!

Without being aware of it, you have already accessed the source. You have had life experiences in which you struggled with a problem and the answer appeared without you thinking about it, seemingly from nowhere. Perhaps you attributed this knowledge, this information, to something such as, "A little voice told me," or "It just came to me." Some people have been startled to perform functions or understand languages they never formally learned. Few have been able to identify where this knowledge came from. You can now: it came from the source.

When it comes to finding the energy needed to change your financial world, you want access to the source as often as possible. Remember earlier discussions about leaving the comfort zone, going into risk mode, having a sincere purpose, and riding the waves? These are all active steps you can take to promote connection to the source. When you put all these elements together and wrestle with the gods all by yourself, you become open to the source, an awesome power that should be treated with the utmost respect. Remember how I obtained my car and apartment? These things came directly from the source, and as such, they contain an extra level of enjoyment, continuing freshness, and uncanny protection from harm. If you have ever been so focused that your energy felt especially pure and flowing, and you witnessed dramatic, unexpected, or magical results, chances are good that you were connected to the source. Instead of viewing these experiences as random events, you can make them more frequent occurrences in your life.

There is no one way to connect to the source. There are various steps you can take to promote accessibility, and certain activities that condition you for this connection. In general, anything that promotes a calm mental state is beneficial, such as exercise, daily meditation, or yoga. Yoga is an excellent physical workout, encouraging flexibility and strength — characteristics so conducive to change. Yoga is also an ancient spiritual tradition; millions of people have done the same yogic positions over hundreds, if not thousands of years. You connect to each of them by doing those positions. Yoga also promotes *letting go,* rather than being attached. Learning to detach is a huge advantage in accessing the source and in recreating your financial world.

Few of us are taught the art of detachment as part of any formal education, and that is a shame. Our society and its institutions promote attachment at every phase of life: you become attached to the idea of your family background, the school you go to, the neighborhood you live in, the class you come from, the job you have, the person you are married to, the possessions you own. Attachment comes with side orders of fear and judgment, designed to keep everyone off-balance.

Understanding what detachment means can be tricky, too, because it does not mean being uncaring or disinterested. Detachment is a mindset that allows things to develop as they should because you are not constantly measuring your progress against a pre-set timetable, other people, or your ideas about results and success. Instead, you allow yourself to appreciate and learn from each step as it unfolds. In the competitive economic climate of the twenty-first century, cultivating detachment in almost everything you do gives you spaciousness and an edge, along with priceless peace of mind.

Learning to detach is a choice you should make, and it is a process. Be patient with it. Start by creating some quiet time for yourself each day. Begin with as little as fifteen minutes in the morning, and do the same thing at night before going to sleep. This process can be called meditation or just quiet time; it doesn't really matter. Find a private place to be still and undisturbed, with no kids, no dogs, and no loving partner. Just sit and allow your mind to calm itself, and watch whatever thoughts come in and out of your mind. Try to be as peaceful as possible, and most of all, don't look to get anything out of it. See this time as an opportunity to just be yourself in your body, without interruption. View it as increasing a kind of stamina or centeredness from which you can deal with all of life's events. It will take time, but eventually you will feel your perspective shift, and you will gain incredible freedom — freedom necessary for you to sculpt your financial future.

By taking this daily time to stop and do nothing, you will increase your connection to the source. If you don't want to do these exercises on your own, most gyms or health clubs offer a variety of breathing and meditation classes. Look for kundalini yoga, too. This is a powerful type of yoga that combines chanting, meditation, and a rigorous physical workout: it helps you breathe deeply, detach, and connect to the source. When you inquire about kundalini yoga, ask if the yoga studio offers *daily sadhana,* which is practice between 4AM and 7AM, a time when the earth awakens and the energy is most potent for healing and creation of wealth.

Gravitate toward things that promote receptivity and openness, or things that please you, like taking a long walk at lunch, or soaking in a hot bath. When you enjoy each moment of the day, you gain a sense of calm and peace of mind that lets you see the opportunities right in front of you, rather than being distracted by illusions of false wealth or security.

The source is not just the energy you need to achieve the goals you want; it's the source of all other life, too. Make no mistake about it — the source has all the power, not you or me. As you become more calm and open, you can tap into the source more easily to achieve your financial goals. Never confuse your personal achievements with what they really are, which is temporary access to the source. Don't let greed and ego ruin your connection.

Monitoring my connection to the source has become second nature to me. It is something I'm aware of throughout my day. It gives me the kind of feedback I need to make the right moment-to-moment decisions. It is the quality — not quantity — of time I spend connected to the source that counts.

I've been fortunate in life and am blessed with some very good raw material, but I am human, too. I'm continually challenged by life's volatility and seeming randomness. You, too are going to encounter challenges, volatility, and resistance as you engage in this new moneymaking process. When it's your turn to address people or situations that cause you difficulty, it's a big advantage to be familiar with the source. Knowing about the source helps you face adversity with integrity and character, rather than complaining, or labeling yourself a victim.

Being aware of the source allows you to appreciate where you are at the moment, instead of always dwelling on the past, or worrying about the future. In an acting class, a very elderly and wise teacher turned to the class and exclaimed, "Why doesn't anybody ever linger anymore?" I was taken aback and not sure what she meant, but she was keenly prescient. Have you noticed how so many people are in a hurry, often with a look of panic on their faces while constantly checking their mobile devices? *Don't rush through your life.* Disconnect from cellphones, computers, television, and e-mail for just one day a week, and see if it helps you connect to the source. What do you sense or feel in that electronic void?

There are so many other benefits to being connected to the source. The source is where the ideas and the resources necessary to write this book came from. I don't say this gratuitously either — because this book literally wrote itself through me. As my connection to the source grew stronger, I also found that things manifested much more quickly in my life. People seemed to anticipate and fill my needs automatically. There is almost no better feeling than tapping into the source, especially since it is unlimited and unending. Better still, it is available to everyone 24/7. Respect it, defer to it, and remember that it's what we all dip into to accomplish everything.

I traveled frequently between New York and Florida some years ago on Song airlines, a now-defunct division of Delta designed to compete with Jet Blue. This was a time when I was taking yoga classes about three times per week. Song had a trivia game played on the back of each seat in which one competed with the other passengers. Many of the multiple choice questions were geared toward popular culture and included detailed sports questions, such as what was the San Diego Stadium called in 2002 before it changed names. I was amazed when I played this game, because I beat all the passengers about 95% of the time, even though I was completely unfamiliar with about 75% of the questions. I was open enough to let the answers come to me from the source.

There are countless other benefits of being connected to the source. You may start to view time in a different light. Instead of feeling time-pressed, you might see time as limitless. You might also feel that you, and not someone else, should control your time on this planet. When I started to work for other people after law school, I noticed how so much time was wasted with gossip and pettiness that led nowhere. I vowed that as I gained more control over my time, I wouldn't waste it on such negativity. I have kept this promise to myself. I project peace, love, and gratitude onto every life situation, and the reality I create reflects these energies.

I also promised myself that if I ever achieved the kind of control over my financial life that I wanted, I would treat people differently when it came to money. I would not perpetuate the "same old, same old" mentality, which usually consists of everything for yourself and nothing for anyone else. This is a vow I try hard to keep, not only because it makes me feel good, but because it promotes a longer connection to the source; I stand a better chance of sustaining the financial gains I have made.

In addition to the enormous financial benefits you obtain by connecting to the source, there are many other by-products. You become a truly privileged person because of your access to a great wealth of knowledge and information. But privilege has its responsibilities, too. Since you have access to unlimited financial opportunity, you may be called upon to actively address other issues that arise in your energy sphere. These situations require someone to take a stand to balance things out. That someone becomes you, because the responsibility to take action in every life situation falls on the person with the most awareness. As you start connecting to the source, you will appreciate how every life event is connected by the same energy. When you lacked the clarity to see those connections, your response to out-of-balance situations might have been to look away, thinking they were not your problem.

When you have more experience with connecting to the source and reaping its benefits, you develop an expanded sense of where your self-interest lies. When inequities present themselves in your everyday life, you'll be prepared to take action to address those situations.

I am not suggesting anything here that I don't already routinely do. I was fighting evil in my own way on September 11, 2001. One of my properties was being refinanced during the months before that date. This property was extremely large and I held a minority interest, so I did not control the refinancing process. When the refinancing was complete and the checks were distributed, my check bounced. I called the property management office responsible for check distribution and requested a replacement check. When I spoke to the woman who ran that office, she blamed the problem on my bank and was reluctant to contact her bank to correct the situation. She made matters worse by being nasty and abusive.

I would never tolerate an employee so offensive, but she was a long-time employee given much latitude by the other investors to run the business. I had sensed her condescending attitude before this incident, but the managing partners rationalized her behavior by citing her efficiency.

After repeatedly coaxing her over a two-week period, she finally agreed to contact her bank and issue me a replacement check, which I never received because she sent it to the wrong address. As a result, I had the pleasure of calling her *again* to request that a *third* check be sent to me. She was even more insulting and defensive than before when confronted with her errors, because she prided herself on being perfect. I tried to remain as calm as possible, but I do not react well to verbal abuse.

I actually received the third check after about a month of delays. Even though I was a minority shareholder in this property, my share of the refinancing proceeds was significant, and the interest lost from a one-month delay could have bought quite a few nice lunches.

On 9/11 as the planes were attacking New York (an evil of far greater magnitude than the one I was challenging), I was on my computer writing a letter to the other investors demanding an apology for my treatment, and compensation for the one month in lost interest. When I told another investor what I had gone through, he thought I was wasting my time and said, "You finally got your money, didn't you?"

I may have gotten my money, but this woman was clearly out of balance and extremely abusive. She behaved as though I had caused the problems, when it was she or her bank that had goofed — again and again. I seemed to be the only one inclined to do anything about this situation.

I received two responses to the letter I wrote: one was an apology from the other bank for any inconvenience caused me when the first check bounced, and the other letter was from the managing partners that included a check for most of the lost interest I had demanded. Although I didn't get all the interest I requested, I got a good part of it, along with an admission that their behavior was not only sloppy, but out of line.

When I started this story, I stated that I was fighting evil. Evil starts small, comes in many forms, and grows when abusive behavior goes unchecked. I was doing my part to prevent future abuse to other people. I know that my action benefited other people, because that abusive woman "retired" shortly after this incident, and no longer works anywhere.

Out-of-balance situations often have exploitative elements, but exploitation is a two-way street requiring willing victims who feel disempowered. The difference that one person can make in any situation is amazing because the consciousness of hope spreads like the consciousness of victimization. Energy of all kinds is contagious and spreads easily from one person to another.

When you connect to the source, it becomes your choice, and your responsibility, to spread as much joy as you can in this world. Sadness and fear are too pervasive and often get free rein in conversation and in the media. Don't look the other way when injustice is knocking at your door. Do your part to live in a life-affirming way. Always stand ready to take action when needed.

Hope and joy are yours more often when you connect to the source, and hopelessness and sorrow take a back seat, or even get eliminated. One thing that always puzzled me about World War II was how people could be such willing victims. I like to think that if I was a Jew in those times, I would have seen the signs and gotten myself out of the danger zone before the situation became critical. When I see pictures of death camps with German guards, I think how the sheer mass of prisoners so overwhelmed the number of guards. If those camp detainees had all decided to fight back, many of them might have died. But if the consciousness of fighting back was transmitted from one detainee to another, the result may have changed. I am aware that many of these camp detainees were afraid, despondent, malnourished, or just wanted to stay alive. What if each of them, while in line to turn in his or her valuables and personal effects, decided to spit in the Nazi officer's face?

Or what if the Jews everywhere, prior to deportation, simply refused to wear those yellow stars that the Nazis required? What kind of symbolism would this have imparted? These were acts within the energy sphere of the people. Having access to guns might not have been. Having easy access to escape might not have been. Having another country willing to take them might not have been.

These actions could have dramatically changed the energy dynamic of that situation. The Nazis would have realized that the Jews and other camp detainees were not going to take it because they were too tough, and there would be no "final solution." That's because the Jews and others would not allow themselves to be cast as victims in the Nazis' sick drama. It demonstrates how *one* person's attitude in each and every situation is so crucial — because it's so contagious for good or bad. The movie *Inglourious Basterds* borrows this scenario in part, and poignantly shows how a small group of Jewish soldiers with a non-victim consciousness terrorized the entire Nazi war machine.[6]

If one person stands up and shows integrity and courage while under fire, when it counts the most, this inspires others to do the same. Thus, the source is not just the place you access to recreate your financial world. It is also the place where you get the strength and determination to hang in there when the going gets tough.

Contrast the huge number of victims in World War II with the state of Israel today. The descendants of the same people who went passively to the gas chambers are now the most formidable fighting force in the world. This almost magical transformation was accomplished by one thing and one thing only: a complete change in consciousness, and a

6. For a demonstration of how the "victim consciousness" played out in World War II, I recommend the brilliant historical novel The Kindly Ones, by Jonathan Littell.

shift in attitude from "victim" under the Nazis, to one of "never again." The people are the same, but their belief system has changed.

Look at the results. In spite of being outnumbered in the Arab world more than a hundred-to-one, the Israeli military has prevailed against the Arabs in every war. The Israelis decided to never play the role of victim again because it was no longer acceptable. As a direct result of that change in consciousness and belief system, their physical reality has been drastically altered.

The same can be said of the Vietnamese. Despite being overpowered on paper by the American military, the average Vietnamese's belief in "throwing off all foreign domination" was so strong that no quantity of American troops or bombs could destroy it.

The message is clear: You can create the financial world you want with a shift in your belief system — then reality follows suit. By staying connected to the source as often as possible, you not only advance your own financial well-being, you become a kind of early warning system for all kinds of imbalances around you. Think about the grief you can prevent in this world by taking action before those imbalances gain strength.

The source is an abstract concept, but there is substantial reason to believe it exists. There's much to celebrate about it: it is democratic (available to everyone), contains all of mankind's accrued wisdom and experience, and never shuts down — but it is only accessible when your energy is tranquil, flowing, and positive.

Use it but don't abuse it.

- The source is a body of unlimited information and knowledge that exists in everyone's mind.

- Tapping into the source is a process facilitated by being calm and open.
- Create unlimited financial growth by connecting to the source, but don't let ego or greed destroy your gains.
- Connection to the source is a privilege that comes with responsibilities.
- Confront the imbalances in your life with integrity and take appropriate action when required.

CHAPTER 13

MAKE EVERY DAY SWEETER

Making every day in your life sweeter promotes and sustains financial change. In this fast-paced world, you might think slowing down and enjoying life's sweetness is not only an unworthy goal, but a relic of the past. You would be quite wrong. You might ask how establishing sweetness in daily life could have anything to do with making money more effectively. It sounds too good to be true, but a sweet life is essential to your financial, physical, and emotional health because it counters the harshness that so often pervades modern life. It works to diffuse the frantic rush to who knows where, and the sense of hate that characterizes large parts of the world. If you replace all of the world's cynicism with sweetness, you are doing everyone a big favor. The ripple effect is huge, and you won't need to numb yourself with alcohol or drugs because everyday reality becomes simpler and more enjoyable.

If you have been experimenting with the principles of this book, you have probably become more generous toward others with your time and money, and noticed how these efforts have impacted your life. Besides doing things for other people, it's important to start doing things for yourself. And I'm not talking about enhancing your lifestyle.

Cultivating sweetness in life opens a connection to all of humanity. Stop and watch people who are obviously enjoying themselves so you can absorb their joy. Their joy becomes your joy, and then it becomes everybody's joy.

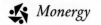

There is a scarcity of healthy role models today who are worth emulating, especially those with no agenda. Many celebrities are out of control, are vastly overpaid, and they behave like the childish monsters all that undeserved attention and money creates. It is rare that admiring a public figure or celebrity gives you any lasting comfort. You may be momentarily intrigued, but more often than not you are shocked or revolted. Take responsibility for creating a sense of self-worth based on your own balance and integrity. In this process, maintaining a constant sense of sweetness is crucial.

Restoring sweetness to everyday life is all about feeling good and taking care of your body, your mind, and your spirit. It's about savoring experiences and not rushing through them. When I spent a college semester abroad at the University of Copenhagen, signs were plastered all over the city: *Take your time.*

Appreciate the things and people available to you in this moment. Approach every person you meet with the awareness that underneath their different exterior, they possess the same human spirit that you do.

I read a very telling article in the *New York Times* regarding investment advice. The article presented a more flexible outlook on investing, and revealed how traditional investment strategies can be unfulfilling to basic human needs. The interviewer asked several financial experts and some wealthy individuals how they would allocate their investment dollars. The traditional financial analysts spit out their version of ideal investing: 60 percent stocks, 25 percent bonds, and 15 percent cash. The non-traditional expert added what was, to the author of the article, a radical notion, which was to spend 20 percent of your resources on experiences. I found it interesting that the idea of spending money on experiences is considered so radical. The writer proposed that the benefits of experiences are repeated over and over again in a lifetime, and that experiences provide seeds for all kinds of ideas and endeavors. One elderly rich person interviewed for the article was asked what, if anything, he regretted in his life. His answer: "I wish I had spent more." Life affirming experiences are invaluable, and they play over and over again in your mind.

When I think about sweetness, I also think about children, specifically my godson, who frequently visits New York. We once spent a fantastic day together going to Central Park, visiting the zoo, climbing rocks, and sailing miniature sailboats. We then met my parents for dinner in midtown Manhattan and walked several blocks to a great Chinese restaurant. I'll never forget what Philippe was crying out as we walked down the street. He was practically screaming, while yanking my hand: "I love it, *I love it, I love it!*" What did he love so much? Walking down the street swinging my hand after a day in the park, knowing he was soon going to eat dinner. These were simple pleasures profoundly appreciated — something we can all emulate more.

Contrast my young friend's attitude with the faces of so many people on their way to work each morning who look as though they are going to the slaughterhouse. It's pretty clear that life is won or lost on a daily basis. You are the one who suffers when your daily life does not provide basic satisfaction, but you also transfer that energy to anyone who comes into contact with you.

How can you bring more sweetness to everyday life? Wean yourself away from the things and people you don't like, and focus more on things and people that give you pleasure. It sounds extreme and simple at the same time, but watch how your world alters when you put it into practice. Observe the energy you let go of and the energy you tap into.

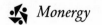

We often need to let go of things and people that are wrong before the right ones can enter our life. Don't be afraid to be without.

Make a list of those things in your life that you routinely do, but are not satisfied with. Take one item from that list and change it, such as the person you drive to work with in the morning. You might have been too polite to say anything for fear of hurting someone's feelings, or maybe you depend on that person for transportation. Make the extra effort to try a different route alone, or with someone else, and see how it changes the quality of your day.

If you feel you waste too much time at work talking with your co-workers, spend more time at your desk just working. Don't be afraid of what others are going to think, since you are not doing this to be unfriendly. Do this because you know wasting time is no longer an acceptable activity.

It may irritate people at work when you don't place their so-called "crisis" on the level they want, but very few stress episodes at work amount to much more than the daily challenges of professional life. Responding as though it were an actual emergency not only adds fuel to the stress fire, it interferes with the fundamental outlook that life should be sweet. *We don't exist to manipulate others or make their lives miserable.* How many people do you know who actually live that way and benefit by it? *You can become one of those people at this moment.*

It's funny to me now, but I used to fantasize about what life would be like if my time were spent actually working toward a goal, rather than wasting it on criticizing people and on things that didn't matter. As I took more control over my work and financial world, I made those fantasies my reality. I found out how to live life unconsumed with toxic and unproductive energy. As you spend less time in those situations, you'll still encounter these attitudes around you. When you do, bless the ground you stand on — you'll have achieved your goal of substantially eliminating this type of energy from your life.

I follow an example that my parents set when I was about ten years old and going to a progressive grade school. My parents typically took us to Florida for Christmas to visit my grandparents, but they extended a two-week school holiday to a one-month vacation. They needed the school's permission for those extra two weeks, and they got it, but the school insisted we do the missed schoolwork in Florida.

A funny thing happened on these trips. We were able to complete two weeks of lessons in one week, giving us an extra week of vacation. As I took more control over my adult work life, I began to think about completing my obligations in less time than was allocated for them, so I could spend more time doing what I wanted. This technique really bore fruit when I worked for myself.

This is just another way to incorporate more sweetness into your daily life, which nourishes your spirit while enabling you to give more to every person and situation you encounter. It helps crystallize your new relationship to work, money, and life in general. Keep this thought in your mind no matter what the activity: *I want to return to the energy of truth and beauty as soon as I can.* This will keep you healthy and youthful, and it will affect everyone you meet. Make the extra effort to only use your energy for things you feel passionate about. When you participate in these activities — as I did when writing this book — pour all the love you have into them.

The world is shifting constantly. In these fast-moving times, be careful how you prioritize your time because it's easy to get caught up in trends you don't even like. Other people (many of whom stuck in unhealthy

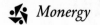

behavior patterns) will not give you permission to make your daily life sweeter, so you must do that for yourself.

- Make every day sweeter to enrich your life in every way.
- Take care of your body, mind, and spirit.
- Share these benefits with everyone, and don't stray too far from truth, love, and beauty.

CHAPTER 14

CELEBRATE PROSPERITY

Having certain fixed beliefs about making money is not only misguided, it's a huge limitation. Many people think you must be manipulative and greedy to get ahead, that you must compromise your principles along the way, that you *must* sell your soul to the highest bidder — or you'll never get access to money and its rewards. Those people are dead wrong.

Don't despair just because some television show about scheming "upscale" people doesn't favor this perspective. It would be surprising if it did, since its interests are more aligned with brainwashing you so you'll buy things you probably don't even want. The joyous experiences described in this chapter are available to anyone, in times of recession, prosperity, or uncertainty — and they are always available.

Being manipulative and greedy is not only counterproductive to your own financial health, its energy pollutes the communal atmosphere. When you realize there is more than enough money for everyone, there's no need for you to sell out either. This awareness is priceless because it allows you to become rich with your soul intact, and to be happy when the people around you have what they want.

For the record, I don't consider myself to be a nice guy, or a bad guy. I have witnessed too many self-described "nice" people treat others in the most despicable way. I just consider myself an American guy shaped by the particular circumstances of my life. In fact, I really don't believe in labels such as "nice" or "bad" to describe anyone. Labels are way too confining, because they don't allow for the fundamental reality of constant change.

Prior to writing this book, I discussed tidbits of my thoughts and experiences with a diverse group of people. Much of the feedback was positive and supportive. Most people expressed a keen interest in seeing the completed book. However, those who were skeptical of some of the energy principles I discovered considered themselves practical, implying that the concepts I advocated did not work in the "real world." These "practical" people often lacked the necessary detachment to see the big picture and the true connectivity of all things. They charted a safe route, and when things didn't make sense, they simply concluded that life wasn't fair. The energy principles I espoused sounded good, but they thought those principles could never lead to financial riches. Or, their eyes glazed over, and they looked at me as though I was some kind of a saint.

I came to find the responses of practical people to be quite predictable. Some needed to put me in a safe category that made sense. It was inconceivable to them that someone could apply my ideas and still have access to lots of money and great life experiences; that was just too threatening to their belief systems. It was hard for some people to believe I had eliminated pettiness, backstabbing, and going through the motions from my daily routine — and that I have not just survived, but thrived.

My motivation in writing this chapter is to demonstrate the quality of experience you can have by shifting your energy to a new paradigm, and that you don't lose out by implementing this book's principles.

There's one caveat before I begin. Describing how I have celebrated prosperity is in no way intended to be a celebration of my own or anyone else's *lifestyle*. It is meant to be a celebration of life. There are ways to increase how much time you spend really enjoying your life, rather than making all kinds of efforts that lead nowhere. Also, the gods demand celebration in a big way once you have played their game with a good spirit, have been yanked around plenty, and have ultimately prevailed.

This chapter is my way of countering the general level of joylessness in the world, its seeming randomness and chaos, and unpleasant worldwide polarization. And as I said earlier, what's the point of having a convertible if you won't put the top down? The same is true with money. *Circulate it for the most joyous and life enhancing purposes.*

In this book, I reveal how I took control over my financial life and my time. In this chapter, I reveal how I celebrated financial success by taking a spectacular trip to Asia. I hope it inspires you to not just accumulate money, but to use your wealth to enhance your life through experiences. When all is said and done, your life is really about the people you have met, and the experiences that you have had.

This was my first trip to Asia, so I tried to make it special. I was fortunate to find out about a one-month air pass offered by Cathay Pacific Airlines. It was perfect for this three-and-a-half-week trip to Hong Kong, Thailand, and Vietnam. (The Vietnam segment was discussed in chapter 3.)

Before I took this trip, I perused a book on spectacular hotels of the world where I noticed a hotel called Amanpuri in Phuket, Thailand. The name Amanpuri means "place of peace." The photos of Amanpuri were enticing because it was set in a banana plantation overlooking the hotel's own beautiful beach. It had separate guest villas, called *salas* in

Thai, which were connected by wooden walkways. The interiors of these *salas* were spare and oh so elegant, with huge bathrooms covered almost entirely in teak; they looked amazing.

I asked my travel agent about Amanpuri, and she shook her head, laughed, and asked, "Do you know how expensive that place is?" She told me it would cost about one thousand dollars a night, including food. She had sent plenty of people to Asia, but had never sent anyone to Amanpuri. She showed me other hotel brochures, but I could not get Amanpuri out of my mind.

There were other factors to be considered. I had just cycled out of the first piece of real estate I purchased, a small rent regulated apartment building in Crown Heights, Brooklyn. This building provided fantastic opportunities to learn about property management and to hone my skills as a landlord.

I accomplished several goals at once by selling that property. This was the only rent stabilized property I owned, so selling it freed me from the paperwork required by the rent stabilization system. I wanted out even though that building provided me with a very good income. Also, I knew intuitively it was time to cycle out, since the New York real estate market was still strong.

I was surprised by what potential buyers thought of this property when I put it up for sale. I had already experienced what free market ownership was like in New York City, and this rent stabilized property seemed much less desirable by comparison. But the income potential of the property was attractive, considering the low rates of return available in banks, or the volatility of the stock market. And Crown Heights, Brooklyn, where the building was located, was becoming trendy, something I had never anticipated.

I adopted the positive view of these buyers, and started to think of this property as a crown jewel. It still took six months to finalize the transaction, even with this mindset. Selling this building involved many ups and downs that came from dealing with numerous prospective buyers who promised what they didn't deliver. When I finally got a signed purchase contract, I rewarded myself with a week at a beach in Florida, and I concluded the transaction upon my return. When the buyer asked me what I planned to do after closing, I told him I wanted to go somewhere I had never been, and was considering Vancouver.

I spent an incredible week in Vancouver several weeks after the closing. I particularly liked that city's magical setting near water and mountains. The city benefited from a fusion of Asian and North American culture. My time in Vancouver prompted me to think about going to Asia, a continent I had never visited.

I started to plan for the Asia trip shortly after returning from Vancouver. I had changed my perspective on the property I had just sold to match the buyers' positive point of view, and a bidding war for the building ensued. I sold it for more than the asking price.

Since the gods had once again been generous to me, I knew it was time for me to spend some money — and a lot of it. When my travel agent told me about Amanpuri and its price, I said, "Let's do it!"

I spent an incredible week at Amanpuri, and even though it was luxurious in a very simple way and often voted one of the best resorts in Asia, it was a huge step out of the comfort zone. It took three different planes and approximately twenty-three hours of flying time to get there. It was anything but "the same old thing."

An amusing incident happened early in my stay as I walked down the beach. This beach was shared with a different high-end resort that cost about half the price of Amanpuri — still not cheap in Thailand where a decent hotel room can be had for fifty dollars a night — but there was a world of difference between the two hotels. Amanpuri was a five-star resort and the other hotel had four stars. The one-star difference was manifested in terms of setup, spaciousness, amenities, sheer elegance, and, most importantly, energy. The feeling of being at Amanpuri was priceless.

I was walking off an incredible beachside lunch and decided to explore the beach belonging to the adjacent hotel. I went over and talked with the employees at its seaside sports center, where one could rent sailboats, jet skis, snorkeling gear, and SCUBA equipment. They were a friendly group of twenty to thirty-year-old Thais who lived and worked in Phuket. They asked me where I was staying, and when I answered Amanpuri, their facial reactions said it all: they started laughing and gesturing with their hands — thumb and middle finger together — indicating the universal symbol for scratch, or money. They did not believe I was staying there. They insisted I looked too young and was not the type of person who could afford it. I suppose I didn't come across like an overfed fat cat, since I was just a guy in a bathing suit walking on the beach. They continued to joke in a good-natured way about how I had to be very rich to stay at Amanpuri. I had been so busy working through and repeating the moneymaking process described in this book that I never fully considered where it was leading me.

My consciousness shifted in that moment. All the energy I had expended had led me to one of the most spectacular places in this world, where I was meant to absorb all the beautiful energy at this place of peace, with a healthy dose of pleasure and exoticism thrown in.

Not only had I tapped into the prosperity consciousness using the principles of this book, I was able to repeat those experiences again and again. I developed faith in this process to let go of money once it came into my hands because my belief system supported the idea that joyful experiences beget more joy. By taking this trip to Asia and only staying in the most incredible five-star hotels, I spent money on the most enjoyable and memorable experiences I could create. These experiences have provided me with perpetual joy ever since. I was not afraid of emptying the till. In fact, the opposite was true. I believed that a new and better cycle was created whenever an old one was ending. I didn't know what that new cycle would be, but I was willing to wait until it unfolded. I realized that life is truly an adventure if you let it be.

More details about Amanpuri: I was picked up at the Phuket airport and whisked away in a brand new chauffeur-driven Volvo for the forty-five minute drive to Amanpuri. The resort had a fleet of chauffeur driven Volvos to take you anywhere. I only used this service once to go into town; the resort was so magical I had no desire to leave. Amanpuri is a group of about fifty separate *salas* and larger villas, set on a hillside in a banana plantation with its own pristine beach. This resort is hilly, so there are unobstructed views of the sea from almost everywhere you look. The effect is one of complete and respectful integration with the environment.

The lobby of the hotel was an open-air pavilion set on one side of an incredibly sculptured swimming pool. On the other side of the pool were two restaurants — also open air. Everything was constructed of the highest quality teak and other natural materials that created a unique air of subdued luxury and sensuality. I was given a chain of orchids as

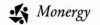

a welcome gift and I smelled them as I was escorted for ten minutes to my *sala.* The flowers' sweet smell was a fitting reflection of where I was at that moment, and of what I was about to experience in the next week.

Although I had seen pictures of these *salas,* I wasn't prepared for their impact in person. The huge bedroom had a low-slung bed and included other beautiful but minimalist furnishings. All the floors and walls were teak, and there were orchids everywhere. The giant bathroom included a huge soaking tub and was connected to the bedroom by sliding teak doors. It had an overall feeling of simplicity — but of the highest taste imaginable. There was one other thing I remember so well when I entered this *sala:* almost other-worldly Thai classical music was wafting throughout. I had never heard Thai classical music before, and its exotic, sensual sound compounded the visually pleasing sense of the space. I bought that CD and now listen to it at home while soaking in a hot tub. When I do, the memories of Amanpuri wash over me again and again.

These *salas* were really one room villas separated from the neighbors by walkways and plenty of space, which created an aura of immense privacy and peace. Adjoining the *sala* was an outdoor pavilion with chaise lounges that afforded beautiful views of the water, which added yet another dimension to its allure. I noticed a welcoming brochure that I sat down to read, which was written in the tone of the most benevolent private host. It gave a brief history of the island and of the land upon which the resort had been built. It suggested, in gracious language, that one had to take advantage of all that this place of peace afforded. It specifically encouraged indulging in the incredible food, the beautiful beach, the sea, and Thai massage. I had experienced traditional

Thai massage in Bangkok before coming to Amanpuri, so I was familiar with that pleasure.

I was only too willing to comply with the suggestions of my impeccable host. After a brief nap, I woke and got dressed for dinner. The dress code was casual and people wore shorts or even bathing suits to dinner. I descended those lit wooden walkways and decided to see what that incredible food was all about. Amanpuri offered a traditional Thai and an Italian restaurant (with chefs flown in from Italy). It sounds strange, but one of the most popular types of food in Thailand is Italian. I decided to try the Italian restaurant that first night and I wasn't disappointed. The restaurant was perched on a cliff overlooking the water. The sounds of the waves crashing against the rocks were hard to resist. I wasn't prepared to have the best Italian food of my life in Thailand, but I sat down to a meal that astounded me. I kept reminding myself that I wasn't in New York City at some great Italian restaurant, and I wasn't in Italy either. I was in a remote part of Thailand where the food had an unsurpassed level of taste and quality. I should not have been surprised, because at the Mandarin Oriental Hotel in Bangkok where I stayed for one week before Amanpuri, I was overwhelmed by the superlative food and service.

I sat there savoring this first meal at Amanpuri with the waves crashing all around me and I thought to myself, "Here is one more unbelievable experience in a string of overwhelming experiences." My entire Asian trip had been just like that.

There's one more detail to complete the picture: On the other side of the swimming pool was an open-air pavilion where live music played for the enjoyment of the guests. But this was no honky-tonk band; it was music unlike anything I had ever heard. Three individuals dressed like Buddhist monks played mellow, exotic, and sensual music — a winning combination of drums and flute that was quite surreal.

My week was spent reading, swimming, snorkeling, and eating fresh fish for lunch, as well as amazing Italian or Thai food for dinner. I had a Thai massage every other day after the beach and before dinner. The massage was done on the low slung enormous bed in my *sala*. I waited in my bathrobe listening to music or just reading, when a gentle knock on the sliding teak entrance door announced a young Thai girl, who respectfully came in and massaged me in the comfort of my own room. Traditional Thai massage, unlike massage in the United States, is an ancient national tradition that involves stretching parts of the body — without any oil — in a way that can only be described as heavenly. I have rarely, if ever, experienced anything as sensual.

I typically collapsed and slept for an hour after getting one of these massages, then got dressed and succumbed to yet another over-the-top dining experience. I have replayed all the pleasures of Amanpuri so many times in my mind, that I now think of the experience as downright cheap.

I am relating the Thailand trip a bit out of sequence. I spent a week at the Mandarin Oriental Hotel in Bangkok before going to Amanpuri. After staying at the Mandarin Oriental, I was convinced that life could never get any better. I had heard for many years that the Mandarin Oriental in Bangkok was the best hotel in the world. And Bangkok, like Rio, was one of those cities I had always dreamed of visiting. I also knew that I had to stay at the Mandarin Oriental if I ever went to Bangkok. The Oriental was a five-star hotel that had a colorful history of more than one hundred years, and it had hosted many of the last century's most famous and infamous characters. When I got off the plane in Bangkok from Hong Kong, where I had just spent three days at the unsurpassed and elegant Peninsula Hotel, I went through customs in Bangkok and was greeted by the following sign: WELCOME TO THE AMAZING KINGDOM OF THAILAND. Truer words were never spoken.

The Oriental was a short cab ride from the airport. My first moments at the hotel set the tone for the experience: pure sweetness. As my bags were whisked to the concierge desk, before I could say or do anything, the most beautiful Thai girl rushed to greet me with the warmest welcome, and gave me incredible-smelling orchids. I looked around, inhaled the aroma, and pinched myself. I was really there on the other side of the world!

I checked in, was given a brief tour of the hotel grounds, and was then taken to my room. My room in the garden wing — more like a two-level suite — didn't disappoint. I had read that the garden wing rooms were the oldest and most storied, with teak floors, a separate writing room for breakfast, and views over the flower-filled swimming pool area. The room was very old world, but it had a thoroughly modernized bathroom with a huge soaking tub that I used frequently. Sliding doors separated the bedroom from the living room, and the bedroom had a most inviting bed with a silk-covered comforter that made sleeping a whole new sensual experience. It was super-exotic, pure luxury. I heartily recommend this hotel to anyone seeking the experience of a lifetime.

My routine at the Oriental started with a leisurely breakfast in my room overlooking the pool — at which time I looked through various sources to choose the day's adventure. Since it was so hot and getting around was a laborious process, I usually limited myself to one main activity each day so that I didn't feel rushed. Most historic spots, temples, and museums were reached by taking the wonderful riverboats accessible to the Oriental. This transport afforded an excellent way to experience everyday life, since ordinary Thais used these riverboats in their daily routines. Locating the sites I visited and getting there was challenging, but it was an indispensable part of the experience. The riverboats often contained large numbers of Buddhist monks, too. I found out that many Thais became monks for one to two years before joining secular life, which explained their calm demeanor. They operated with a different energy than people in the United States and seemed less agenda orientated and more in tune with the present.

One of the most amazing sites in Bangkok was the Grand Palace, a ten-square-block complex of royal buildings going back almost three hundred years. Although this is not considered one of the Seven Wonders of the World, it could easily qualify, with exteriors composed of gold, sapphires, emeralds, and other precious jewels. These royal buildings contained the most unbelievable figurines and Buddhas, many of which were multicolored or made of pure gold. The combination of the heat, these astounding sites, and the thrill of being there, proved overwhelming. Besides the Grand Palace, the National Museum in Bangkok is a sprawling complex not to be missed. I could have spent two weeks there without seeing all the national treasures. The history and richness of Thai culture is something I had never been exposed to. I came away with a deep appreciation and respect for it.

My daily excursions to see the sights in Bangkok left me hot and dehydrated, even though I was there in late November when it was supposed to be cooler. I typically returned to my hotel in the late afternoon, ate lunch by the pool, read awhile, and then took my daily swim. The food and service at the Oriental was unique. It felt as if the hotel staff was reading my mind and anticipating anything I desired.

I had heard how special Thai massage was supposed to be, and after the third day in Bangkok decided to try it. Remember that I spent time in Bangkok before I went to Amanpuri. I had planned to get a massage in one of the Buddhist temples I had read about in a guidebook, but the hotel concierge suggested I try the spa at the Oriental. I didn't even know there was a spa at the Oriental, since it was a separate compound located across the river and reached by shuttle boat. The concierge told me I wouldn't be disappointed, which was the understatement of a lifetime.

I booked a massage for later that same day, went sightseeing for the afternoon, and then returned to the hotel. I took the five-minute boat ride across the river and entered the spa after crossing a long wooden bridge over various ponds and sculpture gardens. I arrived at a unique world of wood, glass, and other natural materials. It felt like entering a Buddhist temple, only instead of sacrifice and prayer, it was a temple of pleasure.

I have visited many health clubs and spas in different parts of the world, and this was not my first massage. Every one of my senses was given immediate notice that this was to be an extraordinary experience. I was given a robe to change into and asked if I wanted any refreshment. I requested mint iced tea. I followed the therapist to my massage room, but the word "room" doesn't do it justice.

Unlike the little cubicles with piped-in new age music that pass for massage rooms elsewhere, this room was about one thousand square feet, and contained open glass areas that overlooked sculpture ponds. It had its own glass-enclosed shower with ten nozzles; even the soap in the shower was unusually fragrant. I felt catapulted to heaven, and I still hadn't had the massage! I sipped the tea and waited for the therapist. He returned and asked me to lie on a mat on the floor. That massage will be forever etched in my consciousness because the energy transmitted was different from anything I'd experienced before. It could be because the therapist looked like a Buddhist monk and seemed so present in the moment. There was another common denominator between this and the other massages I had in Thailand — it felt like pure love being transmitted.

When the massage was completed I could barely talk, let alone think. I managed to stagger back to my hotel room, and after a brief snack, collapsed. When I was getting dressed to go out that evening, I thought, "Why should I be surprised about the day's activity?" I had been in Thailand for only three days, but I was learning a fundamental lesson: be prepared to have your senses overwhelmed each day — by the amazing food, the heat, the pollution, the unbelievably caring hotel staff, the massages, the incredibly rich cultural sites, the exotic atmosphere, or any combination of the above.

My week at the Oriental went by too fast. I began to dread leaving, wondering how Amanpuri could possibly top all of this. I didn't think it could be possible, and in a way it wasn't, though each hotel had its own unique characteristics. As magical as Amanpuri was, the Oriental had a hundred-year history and a real soul that was truly extraordinary. It was a privilege to stay there.

On one of my first days in Bangkok, I took a stroll around the hotel and walked into one of the many custom tailor shops. A sweet Thai girl talked me into getting a custom-made silk shirt; I picked out a beautiful geometric pattern. Since I had never ordered custom-made shirts, I enjoyed the process of being fitted, and actually began to feel like a "proper English gentleman." This was a throwback to a time and place I had not experienced, so it was a lot of fun. It was also amusing because my normal work clothes consist of jeans and a tee shirt.

When I went back to the store to collect my shirt, I was so pleased with the outcome that I bought four more silk shirts in some of the most unusual patterns I had ever seen. When I picked up those shirts, I thought about how great it would be to have some black silk shirts, so I ordered them. When I went back to collect those shirts, that sweet Thai girl knew she had me hooked. I ended up with two silk suits, one in black and the other in sharkskin. Even though I didn't wear suits to work anymore, I couldn't resist. I had never had custom-made suits before, and I enjoyed coming back for several fittings — it made the results feel personal and more pleasurable.

I decided to give in completely to the experience. I asked the tailor to copy my boxer shorts and make five pairs in black silk. The total cost for two custom-made silk suits, ten custom-made silk shirts, and five custom-made boxer shorts was eight hundred dollars. If you could even find the same material, a conservative estimate of the cost to replicate these clothes in New York would be ten thousand dollars.

I have frequently worn the black silk boxers, and I often wore the shirts and suits when the weather turned warm in New York. Here's what happens whenever I put on any of those clothes: a big grin involuntarily sweeps across my face.

You have by now absorbed some of the details of my trip, which I told in an admittedly hodgepodge fashion. My goal was not to impress or overwhelm you, just to describe the experience as part of a process: access the right energy, see that process through, and then enjoy the financial benefits to the maximum with as little friction as possible.

I described portions of the trip out of sequence. The actual trip went like this: three days in Hong Kong at the Peninsula Hotel which was very British and completely awesome, one week in Bangkok at the Oriental, one week in Phuket at Amanpuri, and then two days in Hanoi at the Hanoi Hilton. What did I learn by staying only in five-star hotels? These establishments provided an extraordinary level of service and care, which allowed for a very joyful and restorative experience. I was so inspired by the energy I absorbed that I started to write this book upon my return.

When you tap into prosperity consciousness and mine the source for however long it takes, you enjoy the proceeds at a higher level. Countless movies depict people who connive and manipulate to get that big score in life and then try to live happily ever after on some island. It rarely works out that way. The same is true for people who convince those with advanced age and excessive wealth to marry them. Even if that aged or rich spouse dies right away, the surviving partner rarely enjoyed the proceeds without some glitch. Something is bound to happen — or if it doesn't, the person lives with a nagging feeling inside that they tricked another person out of money. That's not a good energy to carry around because it doesn't promote truly joyous experiences.

It's the energy people use to acquire what they want in life that counts the most. The results will never be enjoyed to the fullest when the energy is tainted from the start — no matter how impressive the prize is.

This contrasts markedly with connecting to the source, leaving the comfort zone behind, wrestling alone with the gods, and facing resistance with a smile. It includes riding those waves for however long they come, and using other people's negative energy, like a goldmine, to push you along to your goal. It involves recognizing that everyone you encounter can be a role model of sorts, not complaining, but being glad for the opportunity to do battle, and being extremely generous throughout the process. When victory is yours in this fashion, the results have a special luster and a protection that can't be bought at any price. This victory has to be earned by you and no one else. Thus, the purer your experience in reaching your financial goals, the purer and more joyous will be your enjoyment of the proceeds *because the entire process is clean.*

By the way, the notion that one can separate one's actions in business from one's personal life is a destructive illusion, because on an energy level it is impossible. Anyone with a modicum of business experience knows this false belief is an umbrella under which the cruelest misdeeds are done to others — by supposedly nice people, too, — all in the interests of business. When you realize that effective immediately, you have exceeded your lifetime quota for trashing others in any part of your life, you put yourself way ahead of most business people, who continue to abuse others for no reason and suffer disastrously from the fallout.

Everything you do in any area of your life, including business, will affect every other area of your life in equal measure. There is no escaping this fact, but most people are not conscious of this, or purposely ignore it to avoid responsibility. If you examine their lives with any degree of honesty, you can see the harm they create for themselves and everyone they touch. By becoming aware of this and with conscious effort, you create a smoother and more trouble-free existence, and you actually get to enjoy the wealth you work so hard to create.

This trip to Asia was a special experience on so many levels: the length of time (almost a month), the exotic places visited, and the five-star accommodations throughout. Life affirming experiences don't get much better than this, but they need not cost so much money, either.

A weekend I spent in Cartagena, Colombia was just as exotic and life-affirming, and the charming, small hotel (with pool) I stayed in cost fifty dollars per night, including breakfast. Celebrate the life you create with life-affirming experiences of your choice.

- Gratefully acknowledge the moneymaking process that you create.
- Enjoy life-affirming experiences to celebrate your prosperity.
- Share your experiences with friends and loved ones.
- Imagine an energy sphere where everyone's life continues to get better and better.

CHAPTER 15

CONCLUSION: WHAT ARE YOU WORTH?

What are you worth? I mean, *what are you really worth?* Is it a monetary figure that flashes into your mind? It's sad to say, but these days you have to be a billionaire to really get noticed by certain segments of society. Is the number of dollars in your bank account what you truly want to be remembered for?

As the new millennium has unfolded, the major financial institutions and/or corporations have been shaken, destroyed, or completely revamped. Individual lives have been uprooted, too. There doesn't seem to be any clear path to financial or personal security, and the cost of certain necessities, like education, healthcare, and housing, can seem distorted and unrelated to real value. Everyone needs to provide for themselves financially, but many people are looking for something more, some meaning that may not have been as important a short time ago; they are increasingly willing to expand their scope to find it. This book can provide that new direction because it addresses energy, a concept that controls everything, especially the flow of money.

When you wake up to how your energy affects everyone and everything around you, it is a total revelation. When you see that the energy you use to make and spend money is so important, you see wealth through a different lens. You realize how dangerous it is to be mindless, but you also see amazing opportunities to shape your financial world.

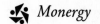

You learn to tune in to a different channel — your own energy channel. Access to that channel provides all you could possibly want or need. If you respect that access, it will last your entire life.

This book addresses some of the more subtle elements and common assumptions about money in a new light — from an energy standpoint. I hope it causes you to think — really think — about your beliefs, and how you treat every person in every moment. That's important not just for you, but for all of us. We all agree that the world would be a better place if there was less air pollution. The world would be infinitely better if people didn't expel toxic energy in the interests of making money. It's unpleasant, unnecessary, and counterproductive.

There is more than enough money to go around for all, even if the world contains huge disparities in wealth. Focus on making your immediate life situation better. Look at money through your own self-imposed limitations, and break down those limitations one by one. Feel and experience the power and joy as you create the wealth you want. Experience the freedom that comes from being detached, and not caring one iota about how much money anyone else has.

Our fast-paced society can eat you alive if you are not careful. Even with all the money many people accumulate, few give themselves permission to enjoy anything fully, to really savor and not rush through experiences. Spending time doing nothing and just relaxing is not usually an option because you have to be productive all the time — or God knows what will happen. *Nothing is going to happen,* except that you'll finally relax and breathe, or take advantage of opportunities that your busyness obscured.

Encourage personal freedom for yourself and for others. For a country that prides itself on personal freedom, precious few Americans truly chart their own path and take control over their own time. The day of the "rugged individualist," if such persons ever existed, is clearly over for most. To be free today requires constant vigilance and extra effort, because there is so much external noise around — and much of that noise contains disingenuous messages. Vigilance starts with very small steps, like re-establishing sweetness in your daily life, and limiting your exposure to all forms of noxious energy — because you become the energy that you absorb.

You have the power to break free and create the kind of financial world you desire right now. You can positively impact everyone you touch in that process. You can become a person who honestly says, "I have enough money." It may not be overnight, and you're going to have to take plenty of risks with a pure and sincere heart. If you make those efforts and persevere, you will be rewarded with such blasts of pure joy and sweetness that you'll know all the effort is worthwhile.

Back to the question at hand: What are you really worth? You are worth the sum total of what you do in every moment of your life. There is no getting around it. That is your true worth. It is also the best guarantee for optimal physical and mental health.

The difference one person can make in every situation is amazing. The ripple effect of your behavior will impact yourself and others for years. As you experiment with the concepts in this book, keep the following in mind:

Have courage and faith. Take a stand and don't give up. Never play the victim. Don't be afraid. Love richly and live passionately. Avoid tribalism of all sorts and strive for innovation. See the constancy in the confusion around you, and just laugh. Promise little. Deliver the unexpected. Watch less. Do more. Savor the moments of your life.

Congratulations! You've just become rich.

WANT MORE MONERGY?

Listen to the radio show at
www.blogtalkradio.com/MonergyLife
(live and archived)

Read the blog at www.MonergyLife.com